Farewell
To
Song Mountain

Books by Veena Schlegel

A Vanished Road
Glimpses of my Master
A Mountain in China
Gulun Kungfu

Farewell
to
Song Mountain

By
Veena Schlegel

Contents

In memory of
my young friend, Ibo Fei

who tragically passed away
on 17th November 2021

*As rivers flowing into the ocean
find their final peace
and their name and form disappear,
even so, the wise
become free from name and form
and enter into the radiance
of the Supreme Spirit.*

— The Upanishads —

Preface

It was a BBC documentary called 'Extreme Pilgrim' that, in 2008, inspired me to travel to the sacred Song Mountain in central China. The photography in the documentary was stunning; the mountain loomed deep, strong, powerful, primordial … and it drew me like a magnet. Also photographed in the documentary was the cave in which the great Zen Master, Bodhidharma, sat in silence for nine years, in the sixth century AD, after which he introduced Zen – or Ch'an – to China.

I had practised Zen meditation in India for about nineteen years and after my Master, Osho, died in 1990, I went to Japan. At the time, I associated that country with Zen more closely than with China. I am an inveterate traveller and am fascinated by new places and new people, but, much as I loved Japan, it somehow wasn't as fulfilling as I had expected and I eventually returned to England. Not long after, I saw the documentary.

In my previous book 'A Mountain in China' I write about my complex, sometimes frustrating, attempts to get myself to this mountain – but once there I knew that I had found my place on the planet. Despite some tough times, my experiences there were far beyond anything I could have dreamed of: richly engrossing and satisfying on every level. From the daily encounters with local people in the village I lived in, to forging deep friendships with young English-speaking graduates, to learning about an ancient way of kungfu, to discovering the spiritual heritage of the region, to exploring Zen, both as the locals understood it and through my own growing experience of it, and to deepening meditations in the energy field of this ancient sacred place … all created a colourful, brightly-shining tapestry woven together from these inner and outer adventures.

And I unexpectedly found that I was on something of a quest. During my first visit to China, I was extremely surprised to find a phrase often used by Osho – 'the ten thousand buddhas' – on a sign in the ancient Longmen Caves in Luoyang. This was intriguing. Why had he used this phrase and where did it originate? I set about looking for answers.

When I published 'A Mountain in China' in 2015 I thought I had said everything I wanted to say (although I hadn't found an answer to my quest), but subsequent visits to my beloved mountain continued to enthrall me and so, encouraged by the many enthusiastic responses from my readers, I felt that this sequel was in order.

Veena Schlegel
United Kingdom
May 2022

1
Song Mountain

The most sacred mountain in China

(Zen) does not want you to create
a certain kind of spirituality,
a certain kind of holiness.
All that it asks is that you live your life
with immediacy, spontaneity.
And then the mundane becomes the sacred.
The great miracle of Zen
is in the transformation
of the mundane into the sacred.

Osho

嵩山

Song Mountain

The pink and orange glow of the rising sun slowly illuminates the still dark outline of the mountain. As I sip my morning cup of tea, sitting here on the balcony, I reflect on my love for this extraordinary mountain to which thousands have journeyed, over thousands of years, to lose themselves – and ultimately find themselves – in its all-encompassing sacredness. Just as they surely were, I am entranced, enthralled, by the primordial and omnipresent power of the mountain and, like them, I willingly allow myself to be embraced and engulfed by its energy.

I have travelled extensively on this much-loved planet but never have I been affected so strongly by the 'spirit' of a place as here. Is it possible to be in love with a 'place'? I think so.

As I yet again melt into the cloud of the unfathomable 'something' enveloping the mountain and me, I know that this will be my last visit here. In the past twelve years I have made my way here twenty-one times, drawn by I am not sure what exactly – at least, drawn by something impossible to put into words. However, like so many writers and seekers, I am attempting here to express the inexpressible.

I was sixty-four years old when I first came here (a time when most people retire from activities and rely on their books or TV's to transport them to other vistas) and now my aging body tells me it is time to rest; tells me it can no longer face the challenges of long journeys, tough living conditions and the daily complexities of everyday living. Of course such challenges are to be expected when one chooses to live in a rural area where almost nobody speaks English, where one cannot function independently and where nothing is the same as back home ... but there comes a time when it all becomes just a bit too arduous

But not for even a fraction of a second do I regret anything of the people, places or situations I have encountered during the past twelve years. Almost without exception the Chinese have been infinitely and unconditionally kind and helpful and have welcomed me with open arms and cared for me as if I were one of their family. But I don't want to outstay that welcome, nor risk becoming burdensome because of my advancing age.

And so, I bow my head in absolute gratitude to the mountain and the people surrounding it for giving me such extraordinary experience at this stage of my life. It is some of these often humorous, heart-warming, inspirational and exhilarating experiences – some of them beyond my humble conception – that I want to record here.

࿐

Silent meditative states were subject to interruptions in my latest living space. During my visits to China I had lived in a number of different places, mostly in the little village of Shilipu, providing a variety of comfort levels and conveniences. My lovely 'Zen' flat – clean, sparse but beautifully designed and efficient, and by far the best place I had stayed in – was a distant memory because my charming landlords, Mr and Mrs Shang, had now turned it and other rooms into a guest house. They were very efficiently cashing in on the recent popularity of Song Mountain as a tourist resort.

Although good for some rueful laughs, this last place lacked most of the usual amenities, but I could ignore all the inconveniences because of the balcony! Being on the second floor it partially elevated me above the ugly, grey, concrete boxes which constitute the housing in the village. I was also above the local community activities and noise and could not be stared at, which was always a relief.

The mountain (and unsightly concrete roofs) from the balcony

Master Wu Nanfang, the kungfu Master who had featured in the BBC documentary and who I had met on the first day of my first visit here, had, assisted by his daughter, Lijuan, who spoke some basic English, helped me unconditionally throughout all my visits. Now on this latest visit he had offered me a place to stay on the top floor of the house that he rented for his kungfu school in Shilipu village.

When they took me to the house early in the morning, I had to gulp down a gasp of dismay – but managed a laugh at the same time. China could always upset my equilibrium. Whereas the ground and first floors which housed the students had been decorated comfortably and fairly aesthetically (complete with bathrooms with hot water heaters and western toilets) – the top floor featured the original bare concrete walls and floors in their untouched roughness. There was a primitive washing area and a shower – heated only by the solar panel on the roof – next to

Shilipu village from the balcony

a squat toilet. I had experienced living with those solar panels before: they efficiently produced boiling hot water on hot summer days when cool water would have been a blessing, but their efficiency slumped to zero when winter came and hot water was very much needed – and winter would be settling its icy hold on us within three weeks. Seasoned from years of living in India, I would have to go back to the Indian system of heating water in a kettle, pouring it into a bucket, adding cold water, then dousing oneself with water from a plastic cup to wash away the soap. I was pretty expert at this so it wasn't a problem.

All the rooms on this top floor were filled with the debris of the old school building and other unknown sources: rusty bed bunks, loads of filthy bedding and mattresses, ragged old clothes, broken desks, books, and piles of other assorted rubbishy paraphernalia. Frankly, it was rather shocking.

However, I knew the Wu family of old and knew that when Lijuan said she would arrange for a room to be cleared for me and have everything cleaned up, it would happen. She could rely on eager cohorts of young students – like an army of little elves – who could be galvanised into doing a clean-up job. Having watched this phenomenon before, I was convinced the kids secretly enjoyed escaping from training and school lessons and doing something a bit different from their rather boring daily routine.

When I suggested playing some music and provided a huge selection of edible goodies from the local convenience store (where I had also bought sugar, milk and a large bottle of water for my tea the next morning), they were perfectly happy shoving stuff around to the tune of cheerful giggles and lots of chatter. Lijuan was an efficient sergeant-major and ordered them this way and that and within a few hours a bedroom and the main living room were cleared, with all the debris stuffed into the other two bedrooms with the doors firmly closed. Some brooms, mops and buckets were brought from downstairs to wash down the walls and floors, after which the place was declared to be habitable. A thoroughly enjoyable time had been had by all.

Taking two of the older boys, I then went next door to Mr and Mrs Shang's house to greet them and give them some presents from England. (The village grapevine had already informed them that I was back.) I needed to pick up the three big bags full of my own household goods – my own bedding, kitchen paraphernalia, a hairdryer and an iron – that they had kindly stored for me in their attic while I had been away. In the meantime, Lijuan supervised the installation of three old 'easy' chairs in the living room, and a double bed in the bedroom, from a room downstairs.

By the end of the day everything was in place, including my 'kitchen' laid out on two old school desks – a source of great interest to the students who had never seen such an unconventional set-up. During my various visits I had acquired crockery (very nice – China was good at 'china'), cutlery, efficient Chinese chopping knives, a rice cooker and contraption not seen in western countries: a kind of electric frying pan – for eggs, tofu and vegetables – with a heated lid which meant I could almost 'bake' vegetables such as potatoes. I could steam vegetables in a special steaming container which was fixed on top of boiling rice in the rice cooker – the steam from below cooked the vegetables above and the juices from the vegetables fell into the rice and got absorbed. Very efficient and healthy. I also made soup, and cooked noodles/spaghetti in the cooker.

After all the hard work everybody trouped up to the school for supper, after which my rolled-up foam mattress (because hard wooden Chinese beds were a torture for me) was retrieved from the school's storage area and stuffed into the ancient van, with me in the front seat and Wenju, Master Wu Nanfang's son, driving. Back in the village he got some more boys to carry the mattress up to my room and put it on the bed, after which all I had to do was make up the bed with my own

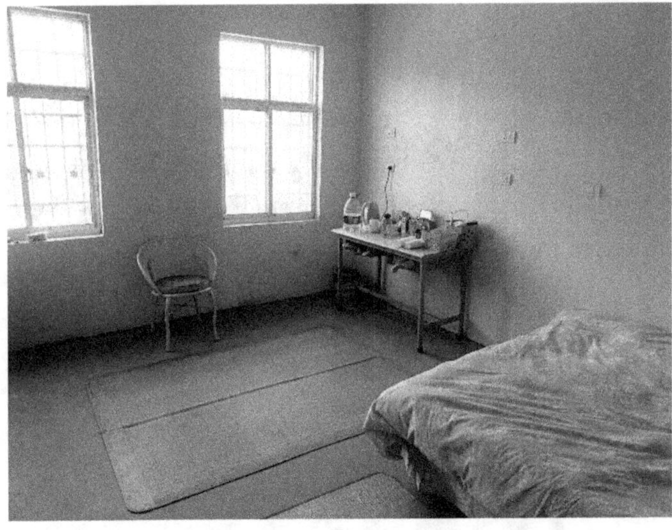

sheets and duvet cover, and fall into it. I was exhausted, but blissfully happy to be back amongst people of such generous innocence, and reconnected with my beloved mountain.

❧❧

The next morning, I was, as I expected, woken up at about 5am when the students downstairs noisily hauled themselves out of their bunk beds and set off up the mountain to the school to start training at 5.30am. As peace returned, I made myself a cup of tea – having previously unpacked my electric kettle, a mug and a spoon from one of the bags – and walked out onto the balcony to drink it. In the east the sky glowed pink with the rising sun and in the west the mountain loomed high in the sky. I felt every cell in my body jump for joy and literally dissolve in wonder as the energy flowed into me. How could I describe this feeling of bliss, harmony, peace? It was simply total, absolute rightness. In only two instances have I experienced this otherworldly state: in my Master, Osho's, presence, and here on Song Mountain.

The balcony experience made it instantly clear that what was unequivocally needed was a special, ultra-comfortable chair so that I could sit here in bliss and imbibe as much as I could of the mountain's magic, despite the dawn chorus of my chicken neighbours who lived next door, only about twelve feet away from my balcony!

The balcony cannot be seen but it is only about twelve feet away
on the same level as the neighbouring chickens' accommodation.
But their murmurings enhanced, rather than disturbed,
my meditations.

A trip into Dengfeng was now a necessity so I braved the primitive shower with its (thankfully) warmish water, got dressed and set off down the village to the bus stop. The villagers, most of them having been farmers until recently, were already up and about, and were happy to greet me with a chorus of '*nihao*'s '(greetings) from the adults and 'bye-byes' from the toddlers who were so proud to be able to speak English! At the bus stop I bought a hot sesame bun from the vendors there and boarded the next bus into town. The buses were now electric so were beautifully quiet and smooth. I wanted to go to a furniture shop where I had previously bought stuff, and then on to the big supermarket at the other end of town. As it took about half an hour to get into Dengfeng I knew the shops would just be opening when I arrived.

I remembered Michael, a French kungfu friend, saying to me once, in a rather embarrassed way, that he couldn't believe how he could sit in a crowded noisy bus going into Dengfeng and be filled with a feeling of quiet peace and joy. I replied that I knew exactly what he meant because I often had that feeling too. I felt it that morning.

At the furniture shop I found the perfect chair – a very simply metal one covered with plastic strips bound around the frame. It would have been straw or rattan in former times. Struggling to remember my few words of Chinese, I paid for the chair but signalled to the shop assistant that I would go to the supermarket and pick up the chair on the way back. I must have got something right because she understood and put the chair aside till my return.

I then jumped on another bus – there is one about every five minutes – and journeyed to the good supermarket on other side of the town where I could buy everything I needed: some cleaning supplies, some toiletries like shampoo and soap (there was a huge choice of products), some lovely fresh vegetables, my favourite kind of tofu, noodles, soya sauce – and sesame oil. I liked to buy the oil in this shop because they made a speciality of selling freshly pressed oil from an old traditional oil press. The seeds were fed into a channel in the press and a stone wheel went round and round pressing the oil from the seeds. A continuous stream of dark, thick oil was delivered out of a spout into bottles held by a shop assistant, who then screwed the lids onto the bottles and handed one or more to the waiting customers. Luckily this was the cheapest oil available – unrefined, and most importantly, free of the chemicals found in the more expensive vegetable oils.

I also bought three plants because I knew from experience that some verdant greenery could brighten up drab surroundings.

Heavily loaded down with my purchases, I then tried to get a taxi. A few passed me by, the drivers often a bit afraid to get involved with a westerner, but finally one drew up and was rewarded for his bravery by my novel method of getting what I wanted. When one pays the price on the meter – for example, thirty yuan (a couple of British pounds or four or five dollars) to Shilipu village – the taxi company takes twenty yuan and the driver gets ten. My strategy was to offer the driver thirty yuan in cash and indicate that no meter was necessary. If the driver was at all savvy, he quickly realised he could then pocket the full thirty yuan for himself. He might have thought that the foreigner didn't know what he or she was doing but that didn't matter to me. I knew that he benefitted from a little bit of extra cash that day and would also help when needed. In this case, I wanted him to pick up the chair from the furniture shop. As it was directly on the way home this wasn't a problem and I arrived home tired but triumphant with my successful shopping expedition.

Fortunately a truant kungfu student just happened to be available, and he helped me carry my parcels up the three flights of stairs and, at my request, accompanied me down to the convenience store to buy the huge container of water I needed. As the owner of the store, my very good friend, Xiaofeng, wasn't busy, I sent the student home with the water – he knew where to put it –– and then produced the large slab of chocolate I had brought for Xiaofeng from England. He loved English chocolate so I always brought him some. I also brought him a pack of playing cards with English landmarks pictured on them. He was ecstatic.

He was such a kind, innocent-but-intelligent, youngish man who had helped me very much over the years because he had the patience, and lack of fear, to try to figure out what I wanted to buy in his shop. In fact, he enjoyed my acting skills – I had once mimed wanting to burn some incense. And he was amused by my drawings for needed objects, for example, a kitchen knife or some scissors or some nail clippers. He and other customers enjoyed the guessing games.

I was happy to do something for him because he had a hard life. He got up at 5am every morning to go to the market to buy produce for the shop. When I first arrived in China he had one of those indescribable old vehicles, driven by a kind of 'lawn mower' type engine with a trailer at the back. He then later acquired one of the new small truck vehicles which I think the communist government made available to poor people to help them with their small businesses. But both vehicles are uncovered so Xiaofeng would get either soaked to the skin or freezing cold in bad weather. He only closed his shop at 9pm, having worked the whole day with no breaks – and he did this seven days a week. During my last visit I was a glad to see that he had bought a nice new van to carry all the goods from the markets, so he was at least protected from the elements. His little business was obviously doing well and he deserved to have some comfort.

My visits to China were not only about the magic of the sacred mountain and its long spiritual traditions, but also about experiencing the light-hearted interactions with the local people. I was always touched by their friendliness, generosity and innocent curiosity. These

Xiaofeng in front of his village store

many small, mundane, everyday events and discoveries seemed indeed to be transformed in the presence of the mountain into something beyond the known.

2
Taoist Temples

Zhongyue Miao

Be still.
Stillness reveals the secrets of eternity.

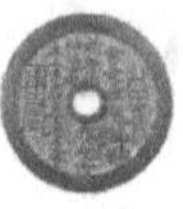

To a mind that is still
the whole universe surrenders.

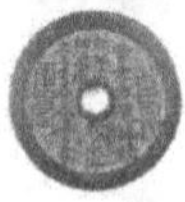

Abide in steadfast stillness.
Attain utmost emptiness.

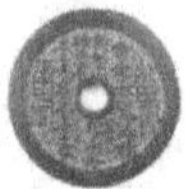

Become totally empty
Quiet the restlessness of the mind
Only then will you witness
everything unfolding from emptiness.

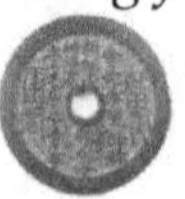

Music in the soul
can be heard by the universe.

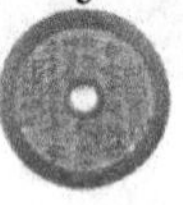

From wonder into wonder
existence opens.

Lao Tzu: The Tao Te Ching

Taoist Temples

Having finally got myself settled in my new abode with my daily life more or less organised, it was time to visit my favourite temple in Dengfeng which was not, perhaps surprisingly, the Shaolin Temple, but a Taoist temple on the opposite side of the city. So when Michael called me early one morning from the kungfu school with an invitation to go to this temple, called Zhongyue Miao, I immediately agreed.

Being French, Michael, was something of a connoisseur of food and did not relish the watery, over-boiled food usually served at the kungfu school. He therefore wanted to stop on the way to the Temple and pick up some *baozi* from our favourite street vendor in downtown Dengfeng. As my usual breakfast was also pretty paltry, I said 'yes' to the *baozi* stop, and by the time he had walked down the mountain (about fifteen minutes) I was ready and waiting for him outside the house in Shilipu, from where we caught the nice, new, silent, electric bus into town.

Going to our *baozi* vendor really early in the morning was one of my favourite things to do in Dengfeng. During the last few years of my visits, the authorities had decided to try to turn Dengfeng into a modern city, complete with lots of shopping malls in which, contrary to the grand plan, the only businesses actually open were some customer-free jewellery shops and fast-food outlets like McDonalds and Kentucky

Fried Chicken, where young Chinese could get their daily junk food fix. Whoever did the market research for the new projects forgot to take into account that this was a poor agricultural area which meant that the locals just didn't have any disposable cash to spend in expensive shopping malls.

Before coming to China, I had of course read 'The Lonely Planet Guide to China', in which Dengfeng was scornfully dismissed as a 'tatty little Chinese town'. But I liked it as a tatty little town! It was honest, real, and had character, with many small shops and rather charming street vendors for whom I was the novelty of the day. Now all the thriving little shops had been destroyed to be replaced by the empty shopping malls and the street vendors had been chased off the streets because they made the place look 'untidy' and were not in keeping with China's new modern image.

One small narrow street had, however, survived the ongoing and

heartless urbanisation. Both Michael and I loved this little hidden-away street, especially in the early morning when the small shops were slowly opening and the vendors were selling the locals their breakfasts of millet gruel, or sesame buns with tofu, or *baozi*. Most people were sit-

Buying baozi from our favourite street vendor

ting about chatting companionably with each other while eating this traditional breakfast fare. They of course knew us because we had been going there for years and, furthermore, they enjoyed passing the time of day with Michael with whom they were fascinated because he could speak Chinese. It was a heart-warming scene that we walked through on our way to our favourite *baozi* vendor.

Baozi are hard to describe as we have no equivalent in our western world. They are a kind of *dim sum:* small buns filled with a mixture of cheap meat or chicken or vegetables, then steamed in huge bamboo containers over a kind of hot plate. They can be tasteless or delicious, depending on the vendor's culinary skills. Our choices were predictably delicious, especially the vegetarian options. The young woman serving the crowds around her worked at lightning speed, but always had a smile for us, especially for Michael! Without us asking, she would move her giant containers around to access the vegetarian option, questioning us only to know how many we wanted. As they were a whole one yuan each (just a few pennies), I usually ordered at least six – Michael more – three to eat right away and three as take-aways for lunch wherever we ended up.

We sat on the tiny stools provided and the locals chatted with Michael as we ate our breakfast. They were so friendly and sweet – I often had tears in my eyes as they connected with us. I think it was unusual for them to see some westerners joining them in this 'tatty little street venue' instead of patronising the five-star hotels where most westerners usually gathered.

Replete with this very satisfactory breakfast, we moved on to catch the No 2 bus which would take us out of the east side of the city and onto the old Zhengzhou Road to the Temple, which is at the foot of another mountain, Mount Taishi, in the Song Mountain range.

ஒ௸

Zhongyue Miao[1] is an ancient Taoist temple – actually one of the oldest temples in China – which I love very much and in which I have spent many hours meditating. It has a much 'softer' energy than the Shaolin Temple, feeling quieter and more meditative because, being less famous, there are far fewer tourists. This Temple is actually much older than the Shaolin Temple: a Taoist shrine honouring the mountain was first built here as early as about 600 BC, a time roughly corresponding to the time of Lao Tzu. As Lao Tzu was born in about 571 BC and lived in Luyi in the eastern part of Henan Province, there is a good possibility that he actually visited here.

I base this perhaps fanciful idea on the fact that historical accounts appear to agree that Lao Tzu was appointed to the office of *shi* (historian) at the royal court of the Zhou Dynasty in the Luoyang area. If LaoTzu travelled from his home town in Luyi to the Luoyang area, he would have had to cross the Song Mountain range by an ancient pass – parts of which are still visible – behind the Shaolin Temple. At that time this was the most used (and possibly the only) pass across the mountain range in this area. This would mean LaoTzu would have had to travel through what is now Dengfeng, and, because of the famous shrine now indicated by a small pagoda called Yaosen Pavilion, I am sure he would have stopped there to pay homage to it.

In Taoism – a philosophical and spiritual tradition which emphasizes living in harmony with the Tao (or the Way) – nature, particularly mountains, are important. Although Hua Shan in Shaanxi Province is the most sacred mountain for Taoists, the area of Song Mountain that I am mostly writing about, was also of great importance for them. Master Wu Nanfang is adamant that Lao Tzu spent some time in this area.

Very little is written about Zhongyue Miao in English so my facts are rather scarce but there is a sign in almost incomprehensible English which seems to indicate that the Temple embodies the Taoist principle of harmony between man, earth and heaven. So it seems it was built principally to worship Song Mountain – although 'worship' is a wrong word. The feeling is more an embracing and an acknowledging of the essence and harmony of nature of which the mountain is a powerful symbol. The energy here is very different to a Buddhist temple as there are no Buddha images and none of the ritualistic Buddhist activities found in most other Chinese temples.

In the central courtyard is a stone stele dating from around the tenth century which shows surprisingly modernistic symbols of the five sacred Taoist mountains (Tai Shan, in Shandong province; Hua Shan, in Shaanxi province; Heng Shan Bei, in Shaanxi province; Heng Shan Nan, in Hunan province; and Song Shan, in Henan province). 'Shan' means mountain in Chinese. At the four corners of this square courtyard are huge rocks on which the symbols of four mountains are carved. A central rock is dedicated to Song Mountain. Each of the five Taoist mountains embodies one of the five elements known in Chinese cosmology and traditional medicine: earth, fire, metal, wood and water. Song Mountain, the central mountain, is associated with earth.

⁂

To be honest, despite the connections with Bodhidharma in the Shaolin Temple, it is Zhongyue Miao, built in homage to Song Mountain, that touches me most deeply. Maybe I was a Taoist in another life!

Michael has told me that he is also touched more by Zhongyue Miao than the Shaolin Temple and it is always a pleasure to visit with him as he seems to fall into the same silent space as I do when we enter the quite extensive grounds. It is really uncanny. It is as if the Temple is cocooned in a cloud of joyful silence which gently engulfs one as soon as one enters the precincts.

As it was still very early in the morning that day, there was almost nobody there except for some monks with their black clothing and strange hats which covered the 'topknots' on the top of their heads. They don't cut their hair, in contrast to the Shaolin monks who shave their heads. The latter also mostly wear grey or gold-coloured outfits. In contrast too, the Taoist monks seem to be friendlier and much more cheerful than their Buddhist counterparts.

We wandered through one of the gates which seems to be dedicated to Lao Tzu into the central courtyard where the energy was so strong that we automatically sat down and floated into a soft meditation which was fortunately not disturbed by tourists eager to have a photo taken with exotic visitors like ourselves, or by youngsters wanting to engage us in conversation via the translation apps on their phones. The Chinese are very friendly and curious but they don't understand meditation and so they have no sense that they are disturbing you when you are sitting quietly with eyes closed. Hence the importance of getting early.

A Taoist monk

An inner courtyard of the Temple

After a peaceful meditation we walked into another courtyard to view a favourite scene which seems to have remained hidden to most visitors. Nowhere on any website have I seen this quite extraordinary part of the temple mentioned. In fact, I only discovered it after my fourth or fifth visit there. (As I mentioned before, the few information boards are inadequate and, when English is used, virtually incomprehensible – hence my lack of factual knowledge about this unique Temple.) On each side of this courtyard are unimportant-looking and uninviting doors, but, if you do enter, you are met with a view of an extraordinarily long hall, with high wooden rafters, housing about sixty large figures, with disproportionally small ones – apparently serving figures – which commemorate former important disciples of the temple. All the figures wear brightly coloured robes. It is an extremely impressive sight although it does give one a rather eery feeling.

Having discovered this extremely unusual place – I have never seen anything like it in any other Chinese temple – I always visited it and found to my amusement that the 'clothing' of the statues was regularly changed, perhaps to indicate a special event or season? It is a totally fascinating spectacle to which Michael and I were always drawn. (In India there are temples where they do the same thing with the Murtis, especially in the Krishna bhakti traditions. In Bali too.)

Throughout the Temple precincts, there are many Taoist symbols, such as the Tai-ji symbol (better known as the Yin/Yang symbol representing the unity and duality of nature) and the Bagua symbol (which consists of eight sets of three lines, broken and unbroken in different combinations, representing natural forces. They are often seen in conjunction with the yin-yang symbol). Both symbols feature in parts of the Temple buildings, such as floor tiles, and metal burners used for the ritual burning of offerings and prayers to the holy mountain. In the various rituals that Chinese people like to follow, they burn offerings of paper, coloured to perhaps symbolise something desirable such as money; or simply as offerings of devotion to the mountain god. Or they hold little ceremonies to make beloved dead ancestors happy by burning pictures of personal possessions, like a house, clothes or maybe a car. The offerings are sent to the loved ones wherever they are via the smoke rising up into the sky.

In this inner courtyard there are many of the ancient cypress trees – some over two thousand years old – for which this Temple is famous, and some thoughtfully placed benches where we sat and ate our *baozi* lunch. Some young Chinese women found us and were absolutely delighted to find that they could converse with Michael. Travelling with him is always an adventure.

On the way out, we gently rubbed the bellies of the four three-metre-high Song Dynasty iron figures originally cast in 1064. They are the biggest and best-preserved existing iron statues in China. It is said that they can cure diseases and prevent disasters, so it is of course obligatory to bow to them and rub their shining bellies. And it makes a good photograph for one's collection.

Saying our silent farewells to this beautiful Temple, we seemed to float blissfully out through the huge wooden doors and straight into the comfort of a providential taxi waiting just outside. We drove quietly through the busy streets, carrying the peace of Zhongyue Miao Temple back to our respective mountain dwellings on the other side of Dengfeng.

❧

A few evenings later, relaxing on my bed in my somewhat basic abode, the door was flung open and in rushed YaJun, an energetic young man, about thirty-six years old, who is interested in just about everything (loves the British Queen) but is especially passionate about anything historical or ancient in the local area.

He had found that I shared his enthusiasm and so was always either sending me snippets of information on WeChat (a social-media-type app on mobile phones – a sort of Chinese equivalent to Facebook), or arriving wherever I was living with some new historical facts he thought I would like. Usually these were invaluable and I learned a lot from him. The problem was that he could speak no English so our communication was via translation apps on our phones. As he talked a lot and was impatient, this often ended up being rather frustrating.

This time he was bursting with some news of Lao Tzu. He knew my interest in him. Through our respective apps, he told me the story about a strange-looking edifice, called LaoJun Tai, at a location which for over two thousand, five hundred years has been associated with Lao Tzu. This place is where he was supposedly born – in Zhoukuo, Luyi County (eastern Henan province), which is about two hundred and seventy kilometres south east of Song Mountain. The present Temple was built about twelve hundred years ago.

The story goes that during the Sino-Japanese war, in 1938, some Japanese officers, on learning of the precious significance of LaoJun Tai,

decided to destroy it. After shelling it unsuccessfully with explosives, they then dropped thirteen bombs on it, none of which exploded. Totally baffled by the failure of their ammunition to do what was required, they gave up and left the Temple alone.

In 1980, one of the military personnel involved in the destruction mission, a Mr Taro Meichuan, returned to LaoJun Tai and told the locals how he and his Japanese cohorts were so amazed that none of their bombs had exploded, that they concluded that the Temple's sacred energy was strong enough to prevent their destructive attempt. In awe they decided to give up and leave the place.

The locals were so touched by the story told by Taro Meichuan that they had it inscribed on a white pillar in commemoration, now encased in glass to protect it.

Also, after listening to this story, the City Council decided to try to detonate one of the bombs which had been at the time carefully buried out of harm's way. Perhaps they were defective? Some bomb experts were commissioned to cautiously uncover one of the bombs and take it away to be safely denotated. The bomb exploded immediately. There was nothing wrong with it!

To honour this extraordinary event, locals put fake bombs around the Temple to show where they had fallen but failed to explode.

How much of this is simply creative story-telling, I don't know. But there seems to be some factual basis to the event (I checked online when I returned to the UK) and anyway it is an uplifting and charming tale, well worth listening to and enjoying.

3
Facets of the Mountain

The Shaolin Temple's Image of Zen

My real dwelling
has no pillars.
And no roof either.
So rain cannot soak it
and wind cannot blow
it down.

Ikkyū (1394–1481)
Japanese Zen monk and poet.

Facets of the Mountain

One of my favourite times and places to meditate in later years was in the evening up on the mountain behind the kungfu school. Sitting on a low stone wall surrounding a large water hole, I had an unobstructed view of the mountain with the sun setting behind it, often providing a kaleidoscope of vibrant colours. It was very silent – only the muted sound of the traffic on the road to the Shaolin Temple could be heard. I was usually undisturbed because early evening was not a time for locals to have a stroll. This was the sacred supper time all over China, never to be missed.

I couldn't, however, quite ignore the pangs of remembering other places on the mountain where I had had more chance of being alone and silent. In the first few years of being here, before the UNESCO award in 2010 which sadly heralded a momentous age of full-scale tourism, this area had remained undisturbed and unaltered for many hundreds of years. Roaming the mountain allowed me to experience total solitude with only the sky, the trees and a few birds as my companions. That nobody on this earth had any idea where I was, was an exhilarating experience of utter freedom such as I had hitherto never experienced anywhere else. It was like swimming alone in the ocean, or flying without tethers high in the sky. And it was a most valuable

lesson in trying to understand what countless Zen masters, including mine, have pointed their finger to.

In his book *Zen Baggage: A Pilgrimage to China*, Bill Porter explains this phenomenon better than I can. He says: 'In the realm of spiritual cultivation, mountains are tantamount to what we call 'graduate school' in the west. Mountains are where people go to make a teaching their own, a teaching they first study with a teacher in a monastery or nunnery, or in the past, in a Confucian academy. Of course, this period of independent study could just as easily be carried out on other marginal land beyond the noise of civilisation, such as a swamp or desert. But mountains seem to be everyone's first choice. The key is solitude. Solitude isn't for everyone, but it is essential for anyone who hopes to go beyond written accounts of the spiritual path or an intellectual understanding of it.'

Perfectly said, and my experience exactly.

ॐ

Back in the present, I looked at my watch and realised that the kungfu students would be finishing off their afternoon training and waiting for their supper to which I was fortunately always invited. I heard the supper bell ringing so I walked back down the hill keeping my eyes glued to the dirt track in search of crystal stones. Song Mountain is a crystal mountain – is that one of the reasons it has such a strong energy, I wonder? – and for years small scale mining for crystals had been carried on there, ending only when the range of mountains surrounding Dengfeng became protected by UNESCO. Over the years I had amassed a large collection of crystal stones which I took back home with me in an attempt to carry a little bit of the mountain's energy with me.

That evening, sitting eating supper with some of the western kungfu students, I heard that they had made a plan to visit the Shaolin Temple early the next morning. I was invited and I happily said yes. Although Shilipu village is on the way to the Shaolin Temple from Dengfeng, it is difficult to get there because there is only the small No. 8 Shaolin bus to catch, and it is always full of locals and tourists by the time it reaches the village. Similarly, it is impossible to get a taxi as they too are filled with tourists on the way to the Temple.

For this visit Michael had contacted a local man who drove a very dilapidated van which, as far as I could tell, only functioned with two gears: first and third. But the man was charming and the cost was low so he was a popular private taxi for the school students, the only difficulty being language. With Michael around, however, that problem disappeared.

Many interesting western people came to study Gulun Kungfu at Master Wu Nanfang's school. I had met many of them online as I was able to advise them on how to get the very tricky Chinese visa, where what was said or not said was very important. In trying to get my own visas, I had studied the options available to most western students and so learnt something of the complicated procedures. It was always a pleasure to meet the students 'in the flesh', as it were.

Two of the foreign students at the supper table that evening were a Belgium couple who I clearly remembered because the man was a well-known saxophonist. It struck me as rather unusual to mix the saxophone with kungfu. They were also very interested in Zen, the spiritual foundation of Gulun Kungfu.

They had all decided to do the amazing, but very tough, long walk across the mountain – one of the most incredible things I have ever done. It wasn't just a stroll; it was a climb up peaks and down valleys on very rough paths with no handrails. Not a walk in the park. Just before the final descent from the mountain, they would pass by the stunning, almost finished, construction feat that is the monastery and temple called SanHuangZhai. I had visited it before but was now sadly too old to accomplish the momentous walk again. I decided, however, to go up in the cable car lift with them because it was an experience in itself. The views were breath-taking.

ॐ

If you want to enjoy the quiet of the Shaolin Temple before the crowds arrive, it is always good to get there as early as possible – so we set off at 6.30am in time for when the gates opened at 7am. The grounds around the actual Temple are interesting and extensive but on that day we went

straight to the Temple itself to enjoy it in silence, free of the bustle of tourists. One of the things I wanted to show the couple was an image carved on a stone stele which dated back to about three hundred years before.

I found this image intriguing for many reasons. The image is not trying to be a symbol of the essence of Zen – such as, for example, the often-seen circular brush stroke calligraphy, attempting to depict the nothingness or emptiness of Zen – but rather an attempt to define its origins.

The explanation which a young guide at the Temple had given me was that the image tries to depict how Bodhidharma fused China's three major spiritual and philosophical traditions – Buddhism, Taoism and Confucianism – into something new and ultimately very different: Zen, or Ch'an, as the Chinese call it.

In this carving the sculptor merges the three figures of Buddha, LaoTzu and Confucius into one, and produces an amazingly modern abstract carving which is possibly difficult to decipher at first glance. It is like one of those trick drawings where, if you look at it in one way, you see perhaps a vase, or a young woman, but if you change your perspective, you see two side portraits, or an old woman.

Looking at the Zen image you first see a figure of Buddha, but by changing your perspective, you see the side views of two figures: on the right is LaoTzu and on the left, Confucius (who, by the way, were contemporaries in the sixth century BC and, according to legend, did actually meet briefly). Blending the three figures together, the unknown sculptor brilliantly depicts a somehow very modern visual impression of the very abstract, almost undefinable evolution of the Chinese concept of Zen.

৵৹৻

My friends had already visited Bodhidharma's cave and the Chuzu Temple, so we set off for the cable car lift which had been installed by an Austrian company with considerable experience and expertise at this kind of thing. I am not sure if I would have been so sanguine about riding on it, if it had been built by a newish Chinese company with not

The beginning of the long mountain walk – still relatively level at this stage.

much experience! That was our consensual opinion anyway. As we soared up to Junji Peak, the view was indescribably magnificent. Stupendous. Worth every risk taken, every penny spent on the very high entrance fees. I walked a little way with the group but when the path got too steep, I said goodbye and turned back to where I knew from past experience there was a convenient place to sit and view the mountain spectacle in awed appreciation. I fell into the usual peaceful silent expansiveness – that by now familiar sense of deep harmony that the mountain always created in me.

In the meantime, the kungfu friends were braving their way up peaks

and down valleys on the vertigo-inducing mountain path, eventually ending up at the extraordinary SanHuangZhai on the highest peak of the mountain range, before making the sheer, knee-punishing descent to a car park below.

The astounding construction feat of SanHuangZhai started about twenty years ago and was completed only very recently. It is the inspiration of the monk called Shi DeJian, also seen in the afore-mentioned BBC documentary, who wanted a mountain retreat to house himself and his kungfu students in suitable solitude to practise kungfu and meditate.

San Huang Zhai can just be seen nestling on a mountain peak

The monastery, hewn out of the mountain rock

The very steep descent from San Huang Zhai to the carpark down below.

Whereas I took the cable car back down to the Shaolin Temple valley and made my way to Shilipu by local bus, the kungfu friends returned home with the man and his van that Michael had arranged to pick them up in the carpark at the base of the mountain.

They later told me that they found it difficult to find words expressive enough to describe how utterly magnificent their walk had been. The mountain enchants many in a million different ways.

4
My Way of Zen

Copy of scroll from the Jufuku-ji Temple, Kamakura, Japan.

My Way of Zen

As a young teenager, I was inspired by a demonstration of traditional Japanese flower arrangements called *Ikebana*, given by a softly-spoken, unassuming and rather beautiful Japanese woman. Her quiet presence, and the flower images she created – simple, clear and uncluttered – struck a chord within me. From then onwards I developed an interest in eastern, specifically Japanese, cultures which, however, remained vague and unfocussed until I arrived in India in early 1972.

There I received a jolt when that hitherto vague interest suddenly zoomed into sharp focus as I listened to a discourse on Zen given by the recently met eastern mystic, Osho. After a few more discourses on the subject, I underwent some kind of shift – almost a seismic one – because although I didn't fully understand, I somehow knew that his indefinable, intangible words were very clearly pointing me in a direction that would be my way, my life, from then onwards.

Despite being born into a Jain family, Osho was for me a Zen Master, and his many discourses on Zen over the next twenty years sank deep into my soul. In the presence of his extraordinary brilliance, I was transformed; I followed him into unknown realms and got glimpses of the ultimate state a human being can reach. But so far away was I from reaching that state myself that, after he died, I knew I still had much inner work to do, and so I decided to go to Japan which was the country I associated with Zen at that time. All those years of meditating with

Osho and imbibing so much of what he said and indicated, perhaps gave me a certain level of understanding and perception without which I probably could not have been able to delve deeper into my own self, aided by the supportive Zen ambience of Japan – and, later on, China

∾

When I went to Japan, in 1990, I fortuitously arrived in a small town, south of Tokyo, called Kamakura. I knew nothing about this place except that there were a few friends living there and that it felt good – right, in some way. Once settled in a rather cute little flat, I managed to get an English-teaching job in nearby Yokohama and also acquired some private English students who came to study in my home.

One of these students was a very intelligent, very perceptive woman who wanted to improve her English language skills. These were already quite good as she was a medical-ethics lawyer and was required to read many western publications for her job. She was also deeply interested in Japanese culture and, sensing my interest, decided to 'educate' me about this topic. I was a very willing student.

One day she invited me to accompany her and her son and his girlfriend to experience a festive tea ceremony in a nearby temple called the Jufuku-ji Temple.

Jufuku-ji Temple

The author with her student in Jufuku-ji Temple in 1992

The ambience was ancient and serene, and as I entered the main building, I stopped suddenly in front of a scroll in the typical ornamental niche found in buildings all over Japan. The scroll showed the characteristic circular Zen Enso, with some calligraphy below it. I asked my student to translate the calligraphy. This is what she said:

> *The emptiness of the full moon*
> *reflects the Zen mind.*

I was stunned. In a few words, this calligraphy summarised just about everything I had understood about Zen – from my teenage discoveries to twenty years of listening to, and meditating with, Osho.

As I have mentioned before, Zen is difficult to explain – perhaps more difficult than any other spiritual path. Using the conventional words of 'emptiness' and 'nothingness' conveys no meaning, and yet that is exactly what Zen is: pure emptiness which contains, however, the supreme essence of existence. And the image of a full moon is used the world over to try to explain something of the mystical, mysterious, other-worldly unknowns to which many aspire.

A man or woman of Zen is pure light, pure clarity, pure compassion, pure awareness, pure truth. This is what I felt Zen to be – and consequently for me there is no other way but Zen.

All this flashed through my mind in a few seconds but my student was perceptive enough to see that my response was profound and asked me to explain what the scroll and her translated words meant to me. I tried – but despite her interest in culture and the knowledge that Zen was deeply embedded in the Japanese psyche, I could sense that she had no actual 'spiritual' or existential connection with it. But I was deeply touched when about six weeks later she came to her lesson at my flat carrying a long cylindrical parcel, beautifully wrapped in the Japanese style. When I carefully unwrapped the gift, I found that it was a copy of the scroll I had seen in the Jufuku-ji Temple. She explained that she knew a quite famous calligrapher and had commissioned him to make this scroll for me. I was moved beyond words – she was so kind, so perceptive, so original. It is surely one of the most precious gifts that I have, to this day, ever received. I have it still.

৵৹৵

Many years later I found out more about the significance of this rather obscure Jufuku-ji Temple. Despite Osho frequently mentioning the name 'Rinzai', I could never figure out where exactly this person fitted into the Zen picture, and it was not until about six years ago, when I came across a book called *Zen's Chinese Heritage*, written by Andy Ferguson, that I found the answer. In the index at the back of this remarkable book, he has given a list of Chinese Zen masters and their comparable Japanese names. And vice versa. There I found that the name 'Rinzai' was the Japanese name of a Chinese Zen master called Linji Yixuan, whose lineage can be traced back to the last Zen Patriarch, Huineng. Linji Yixuan lived in the ninth century – his birthdate is unknown but he died in 866 AD.

For hundreds of years, Japanese monks had been travelling to China, intent on studying the many Buddhist scriptures now becoming available there due to the huge growth of Buddhism. There is an imposing statue of a Japanese monk, dated around 800 AD, in the White Horse Temple near Luoyang.

Statue of a Japanese monk

In 1187 a Japanese Buddhist monk called Myoan Eisai (1141 – 1215), drawn to something that he had vaguely heard about called Zen, arrived at Linji Yixuan's monastery near the city of Shijiazhuang, in Hebei Province, and studied there for four years until he was initiated into the Linji School of Zen Buddhism or, to give it its Japanese name: the Rinzai School of Zen Buddhism.

Visiting Linji Yixuan's monastery in Shijiazhuang, Hebei Province, with my friend, Yujie Zhao

The Great Hall in the monastery

Eisai then returned to his home in Kyushu, Japan, to introduce what he had learned about Zen, and also to cultivate some green tea plants from seeds he brought with him. He thus introduced green tea as well as Zen to Japan.

However, in about 1199, he was invited by the wife of the famous Minamoto no Yoritomo, who established the Kamakura Shogunate, to be the founding abbot at the Jufuku-ji Temple which she had set up as a memorial to her dead husband. Zen thus had the support of ruling Japanese families and flourished throughout the country.

It was also in Kamakura that the nun, Chiyono, famously became enlightened when the bottom fell out of her bucket and the reflection of the moon disappeared. In the poem that she wrote after the event, she said *'No more water, no more reflections of the full moon in the water – emptiness in my hand.'*

Of all the places I could have arrived at in Japan, I had ended up in the town most associated with Zen. I found this quite extraordinary.

ॐ

Because I unfortunately became very ill in Japan, I returned to England to have some necessary medical treatment.

Back in the land of the BBC, and having recovered my strength and physical well-being, I was absolutely ready to move on with my life, both secular and spiritual, when in 2008 I saw a documentary called 'Extreme Pilgrim' which was about an English vicar who travelled to the magnificent and silent Song Mountain in Henan Province, to try to discover more about Zen. Further confirmation, if any was needed, of my interest in this breathtakingly beautiful place happened when I heard the very simple, unsophisticated but insightful explanation of Zen by Master Wu Nanfang. Speaking with the stunning mountain as a backdrop, the soaring birds singing their songs, the wind swaying the trees, and the students silently doing the daily chores, he quietly said that Zen was a harmonising of oneself with nature, becoming one with it, accepting changes, not hanging on to anything, being silently and peacefully relaxed and carefree.

Screen shot from the documentary of Master Wu Nanfang talking to the English vicar, Peter Owen-Jones

He touched me with his simplicity, and at the end of the documentary I knew with total certainty that this was where I had to go to continue my journey. England was not my place.

And so I went to China. The rest, as they say, is history – and it is something of that history that this and my previous book is about.

അൟ

With Zen, even though there may be some scriptures to read, certain temples to meditate in, and a kind of simple ritualistic approach to daily life, really there is nothing to grasp hold of. It is a matter of turning inwards, looking in instead of out, until one reaches a certain point where one's being resides continuously in an inner silent and empty space while at the same time being totally aware of everything and everyone around one. Strong and secure in this pure emptiness, one's being can expand further and further outwards to encompass not only the immediate surroundings, but the farthest stars of the infinite universe. Now all fear drops, life and death lose their relevance and one enters the eternity to which all the great masters – LaoTzu, Buddha, Christ, Bodhidharma, Dogen, Rinzai, Thich Naht Hanh, Osho and so very many more – have pointed.

The ways are different; the end is the same

Sitting silently alone on Song Mountain, far from any crowds, I slowly tried to actualise all that I had learned and imbibed from so many sources, knowing that only when this all became my own experience, my own actuality, my own truth and no-one else's, would I reach the ultimate state. Thus, as it did for so many others before me, the mountain became my solace, my joy and my sacred guide.

5
The Six Zen Patriarchs

Bodhidharma, Huike, Sengcan, Daoxin, Hongren, Huineng

Hsin Hsin Ming

The Great Way is not difficult
for those who have no preferences.
When love and hate are both absent
everything becomes clear and undisguised.
Make the smallest distinction, however,
and heaven and earth are set infinitely apart.

If you wish to see the truth
then hold no opinions for or against anything.
To set up what you like against what you dislike
is the disease of the mind.
When the deep meaning of things is not understood,
the mind's essential peace is disturbed to no avail.

The Way is perfect like vast space
where nothing is lacking and nothing in excess.
Indeed, it is due to our choosing to accept or reject
that we do not see the true nature of things.

Sengcan, the Third Zen Patriarch

The Six Zen Patriarchs

Zen is forever non-serious and playfully appreciative of many things, and so I entered totally into my life lived in the benevolent shadow of Song Mountain – with the many innocent and generous gestures by local people, the joy of unexpected events, and the fascination of seeking out the sacred history of the mountain and all that it has meant to so many devoted seekers over thousands of years. There are vast gaps in this history, because China's past has been a turbulent one, resulting in the loss of countless historical records. This is particularly true of China's spiritual past, because so often successive emperors or warlords suddenly decided that one particular path, or another, should be wiped out. Tragically this is ongoing today.

One further local factor was the great fire in the Shaolin Temple in 1928 when the buildings were almost totally destroyed and the huge library, containing so many local historical records, was burnt to the ground. The Temple was an extremely important seat of learning before this catastrophic fire. It is because of tragedies like this and others – for example the wholesale persecution of Buddhism from 574 to 578, and the consequent destruction of Buddhist records of all descriptions – that so few historically verifiable facts are known about these early spiritual leaders and philosophies in China.

Of compelling interest to me, therefore, was the challenge of piecing together many snippets of information from very diverse sources, into an admittedly unintellectual, unscholarly history of the six Zen Patriarchs – especially Bodhidharma. My history is a personal one, yet I felt it rings true on many levels because so much of it is based on findings gathered from people and places around me – places which I have actually visited. Most of the photographs are mine. I am also able to relate much of it to what I had learned from Osho, for whom the spiritual significance of what these masters were imparting was of far greater importance than mere historical facts and figures.

Delving into the past of these Zen masters has become a kind of joyful pilgrimage for me, satisfying and fulfilling.

Bodhidharma (c.450 - c.600)

Of course, we have to start with this enigmatic enlightened being who has captured the hearts of so many people the world over.

Bodhidharma seems to have been sent to China from south India by his Master – an enlightened Buddhist woman called Prajñātārā – and arrived in southern China around the end of the fifth century. After three years in southern China, where he must have learnt Chinese, he ended up on Song Mountain in Henan province in central China. Here he famously meditated for nine years in a cave on the top of a mountain called Wuru Peak. When he emerged, he started to teach a new form of Buddhism called Zen – or Ch'an in Chinese – in the Chuzu Temple in the Shaolin Temple grounds.

Traditional Buddhism was already prevalent in China because travelling Indian monks had brought scrolls of Buddhist scriptures into China as early as 67 AD.

I arrived in Dengfeng, a small town in the foothills of Song Mountain in Henan Province, central China, on the evening of September 30th, 2008. At breakfast in our unexpectedly clean and comfortable hotel, the young Chinese woman who had helped me and my friend with arrival arrangements, suddenly appeared and asked us if we wanted to visit the Shaolin Temple valley and climb one of the paths up the mountain to see the famous, newly-built temple, SanHuangZhai. Of course we did!

The whole journey was one of mystical magic, but the thing that most struck me was when someone pointed to another mountain peak and said the word 'Bodhidharma'. My heart leapt. This was what I had come for. We could just about make out the cave in which he had sat for nine years on the opposite mountain side – the aforementioned Wuru Peak. It was immediately very clear where I was going next.

Our charming hostess agreed to take us up to the peak and the cave (in Chinese: Damo Dong) the following day. It was a very steep climb up the mountainside to the peak but we finally arrived at the small cave, still mercifully free of the horrendous tourist trappings which materialised during the next few years. There was just enough space inside for my friend and I to sit, alongside a nun from the small Chuzu Temple at the base of the peak. Sitting in meditation in the cave, the energy felt strong and Bodhidharma's enlightenment was tangible and omnipresent.

The views from the cave of the thickly forested, eternally silent Song Mountain range were stupendous.

✂⚬✂

Floating back down the steep steps, we returned to the valley in which the famous Shaolin Temple was situated. It was still fairly early in the morning and the place wasn't yet overrun with local tourists so I was able to spend some time gazing at the stone stele mentioned in a previous chapter which depicted the symbol of Zen. The theory was that Bodhidharma combined elements of these three spiritual philosophies – Buddhism, Taoism and Confucianism – to create Zen. In my experience

The entrance to Bodhidharma's Cave

The Cave

The way down, back to the Chuzu and Shaolin Temples

this was a rather simplistic explanation – but for years I had had the benefit of sitting and listening to Osho talk about the mysteries of Zen.

We next saw another stone stele, also encased in protective glass, which depicts a kind of iconic image of Bodhidharma, complete with the famous ferocious expression, the hypnotic bulging eyes and the earrings. It was difficult to take a photo of the image because so much was reflected in the glass, but on the other hand, the reflections added to the aesthetics of the photograph. Later I was to find that this image was present just about everywhere in Dengfeng.

Years previously, before the image was encased in glass, a kind of resin copy had been made of it from which many copies were printed and then sold as scrolls – similar to how people do 'brass rubbings' of carvings in western churches. Now, however, with improved modern printing methods, the image is printed out and can be found in many buildings, often over personal altars. Master Wu Nanfang has this image of Bodhidharma on a large scroll over his altar in his meditation room. Bodhidharma is much loved and worshipped in the Song Mountain area.

I am rather skeptical, however, about the Shaolin Temple's apparent devotion to Bodhidharma or Damo, as the Chinese call him. It seems to me that Buddha is more important to them, and the inclusion of Bodhidharma is just a useful tourist attraction. While Buddha statues feature in many Halls in the Temple, there is only one statue of Bodhidharma and it is relegated to a less significant Hall.

Possibly one of the reasons for Buddhism being so popular in China is that it is easier to 'grab hold of' than Zen because it has many scriptures to teach, study and discuss, and rituals – often attractive and heart-warming – to practise. There are also many festivals to celebrate during which people enjoy coming together to socialise and worship. In contrast, the essence of Zen is 'emptiness or nothingness', which is difficult for many people to understand.

Iconic mage of Damo on an old stone stele. A reflection
of another part of the temple can be seen

In a small side Hall in the Temple, usually locked, there is a rather mysterious rock, also encased in glass, which was supposedly cut out of the wall of the Cave up on Wuru Peak and brought down and enshrined in the Temple because apparently the shadow of the seated, meditating Bodhidharma is embedded in the stone. If you are fortunate enough to gain access to this side Hall you can narrow your eyes, squint a bit, and exercise your imagination to maybe see the shadow.

For me, of far more significance in my quest for the real Bodhidharma, is the small nunnery about one and a half miles from the Shaolin Temple at the base of Wuru Peak, known as the Chuzu Temple. With the chauvinistic mind-set of the abbots of the Shaolin Temple, this rather shabby little temple has been side-lined and is now seldom visited by the hordes of tourists flocking to the Shaolin valley. But according to Andy Ferguson, who wrote the very detailed *Tracking Bodhidharma*, it was here that Bodhidharma first gave his discourses on Zen. He largely ignored the more popular Shaolin Temple.

The entrance to the Chuzu Temple

Only two years ago I made a surprising discovery. Somebody had sent me a link to a small blog which showed some photos taken by some Japanese tourists in the Shaolin Temple around the turn of the twentieth century, before the destructive fire. Here I saw an image of Bodhidharma that I had never seen before. It was intriguing because he looked much more Indian than Chinese. But nowhere in the Temple complex had I seen either a statue or a painting that resembled this photo.

An old photo of Damo taken by a Japanese tourist around 1900

However, in 2018, I was again visiting the little Chuzu Temple because I love it (it has a deeply peaceful energy which is drastically missing from the more popular Shaolin Temple) and for the first time in all my visits, the small central Hall was open. Stepping up to the entrance I was stunned to see a statue of Bodhidharma which resembled the image in the old Japanese photograph. This was a real discovery. I could also see the faint paintings on the walls which Andy Ferguson talked about. He said they depict Bodhidharma giving his discourses on Zen to crowds of followers.

Very near the little Hall there was a fiercely vigilant nun who was suspiciously watching my every move and I knew she would strongly object if I took photographs. (I am aware that it is considered to be disrespectful to photograph shrines inside a temple.) I did, however, manage unobtrusively to snap a few with my phone. I asked her if I could go inside to have a closer look at the wall paintings but she was quite vehement in her refusal.

A never-before seen image of Damo looking more Indian than Chinese

Old wall paintings showing Damo giving discourses in this temple

With these discoveries, it does appear that Damo was associated more with the quietly secluded Chuzu Temple than the more famous, dominant, very noisy and busy Shaolin Temple.

And I remember Osho referring to Bodhidharma and the Shaolin valley when he spoke about a previous life-time, fourteen hundred years ago. He said:

I had gone there, but I had not time enough to stay in the temple, because the right time is in the middle of the night – when he had become enlightened. And particularly on a full-moon night in a certain month, if you stay in the temple, in the middle of the night, there is every possibility that either you will hear the laughter or you will start laughing.

It is my feeling that Osho was talking about the Chuzu Temple. It is situated in a very silent forested area of the Shaolin valley. I did stay there in a little guest house for a few days just to sit silently in the middle of the night in the light of a very bright full moon, and I think I did hear Bodhidharma laughing! Certainly I started laughing myself at the wonder of it all.

৵৽

As I mentioned before, images of Bodhidharma, both paintings and statues of all descriptions, are everywhere in the Song Mountain area. I found an evocative small statue in a popular tea shop in Dengfeng and a quite stunning statue in the gorgeous FaWang Temple high up on another mountain peak.

But it was a trip to Bodhidharma's tomb between Luoyang and Sanmenxia, on the way to Xi'an – the start of the old Silk Road – that really excited me. The current tomb was rebuilt in 1395 following the destruction of the original one, built in about 538. The original temple

Statue of Bodhidharma in the FaWang Temple

that Bodhidharma had lived in had also been destroyed, but very recently a new temple complex has been built to protect the tomb and other relics.

ॐ

I went there with Master Wu Nanfang, his daughter, Lijuan, and a friend. Unfortunately Lijuan's English skills are not enough to explain anything complex, so it was a rather frustrating time for me because I wanted to know so much but nobody could tell me any details.

For example, I was taken to see an ancient-looking stone stele inside a small temple which everybody got very excited about. I of course got the word 'Damo', but beyond that, I had no idea what I was looking at that justified so much enthusiasm. Everybody took many photographs and indicated that I should do the same – which I obediently did. But why, I didn't know.

The mystery was only solved years later when I read Bill Porter's *Zen Baggage*. In a chapter about Bodhidharma's tomb, he reproduced an image, perhaps a kind of 'rubbing' of a stone stele in the small temple? My little grey cells lit up! Was this that mystery stele I had seen so many years before? I found the photos I had taken, compared them and, eureka, it was! Bill Porter explains the significance: the stele shows probably the first image of Bodhidharma that exists. It was carved on the stone about the same time as the original tomb was built at the time of Bodhidharma's death.

Bodhidharma has been called the First Zen Patriarch and, because of Osho's love and obviously deep connection with him, much of my own personal focus was on him. But Bodhidharma began a lineage which descended through five more great Zen Masters or Patriarchs and I was deeply intrigued to delve into whatever information I could discover about them as well.

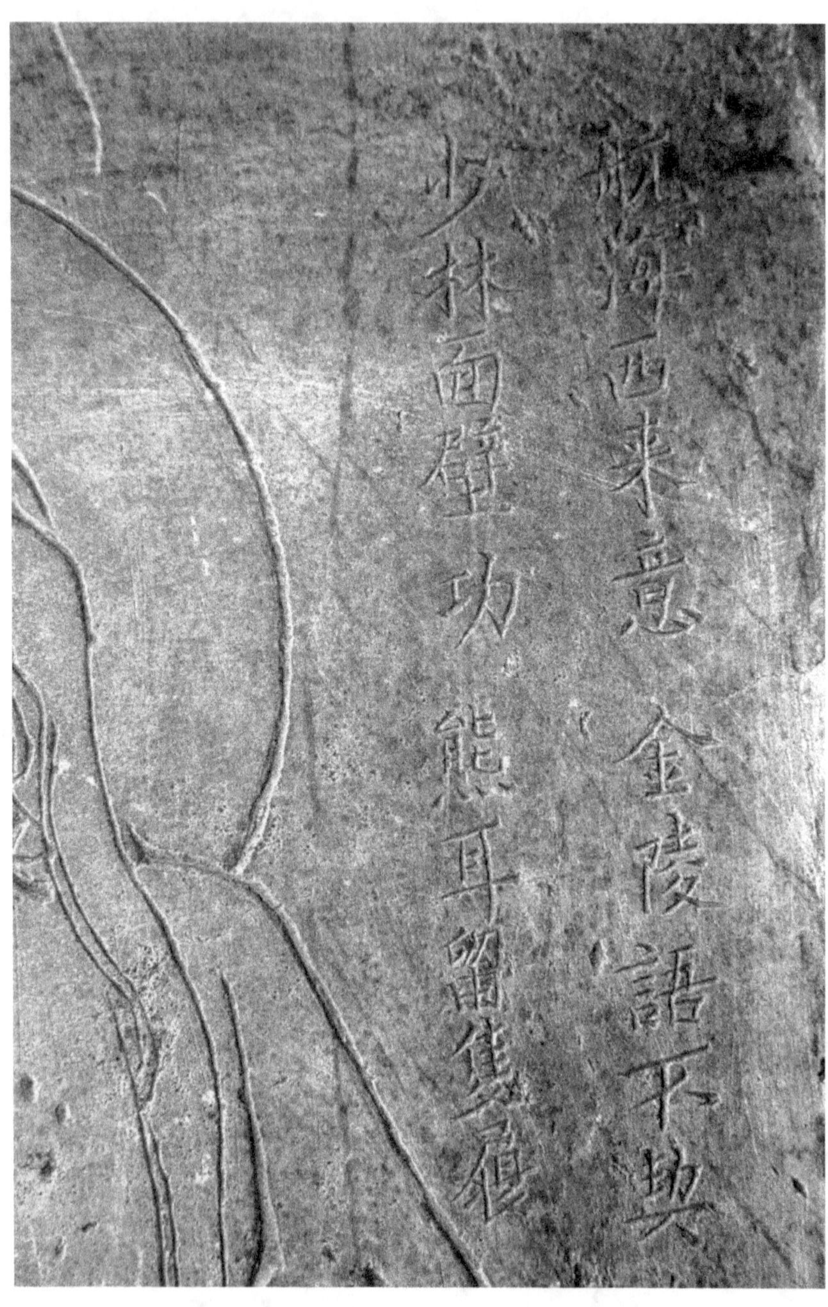
祖師西來意　金陵語不與
少林面壁功　能耳留隻履

Huike (487–593)

Probably most people know about Huike because of the popular story describing how he cut off his left arm to persuade Bodhidharma to accept him as a disciple. There does seem to be some historical basis to this story as it is told in different places in different ways. Interestingly, monks in the Shaolin Temple sometimes use only one hand in the 'namaste' (greeting) gesture, as a nod to Huike who could only use his one hand. Very little else is known about Huike except that he left the Shaolin Temple area after Bodhidharma left and wandered around China. But I have discovered a few bits of information from Chinese friends.

I have previously mentioned meeting the very interesting young man called Ya Jun who is passionate about local history and found a kind of 'kindred spirit' in me because I too wanted to learn as much as possible. As I said, he spoke no English, so our communications were limited to the respective translation apps on our phones. These apps were all right for everyday language but when we got into the realms of spiritual history, they were useless. Despite his enthusiasm, therefore, Ya Jun was only able to share a fraction of what he probably knew.

One day Ya Jun came to my flat in Dengfeng with a tatty old book and enthusiastically showed me two paintings of Huike, which I immediately photographed. I was very excited because these were the first images of Huike I had ever seen. I thought that because they were in a very old Chinese book, I would have a 'scoop'! How exciting it would be to acquire unseen images of Huike! But later I was disappointed to find they were both online.

I was especially curious about the second image – of Huike resting on a tiger – and finally discovered that it was actually based on a story

mentioned by another well-known Zen Master, Dogen.

When talking to his disciples, Dogen told the story of Huike's courage while he waited outside Bodhidharma's cave in the freezing snow and how he cut off his arm to convince Bodhidharma that he was worthy of being a disciple. Dogen said that Huike remembered *'how past bodhisattvas practiced without thinking of their own bodily life, such as the bodhisattva who offered himself to a hungry mother tiger to help her feed her seven cubs. Then Huike thought to himself, "Ancient people with great capability and determination were like that, then who am I?"'*

On reading Dogen's words, the story of the bodhisattva and the tiger seemed familiar, but I couldn't place it until Dhiren Townley, the much-appreciated editor of this book, remembered that the story is told in the Jataka Tales about Buddha, who, in a past incarnation, offered his body to a hungry tiger mother to stop her eating her newly-born cubs. Remembering this story, Huike was inspired to be brave enough to cut off his arm. And in the few rare images that exist of him he is often depicted with a tiger.

৵৽

During one of my early visits to China I found out that there was a small, rather dilapidated, house on Mount Shaoshi which is on the opposite side of the valley from Bodhidharma's cave on Wuru Peak. Huike apparently lived here while he was a disciple of Bodhidharma. I don't know much more than that. But my fantasy was that, because the cave could be seen from Huike's house, he could have waved or bowed to his Master each day on the opposite side of the valley!

Then, a few years ago, I met a very interesting young Chinese woman called Sara. (Some modern Chinese give themselves western names.) Although she spoke good English, she had never talked with a westerner before, so she was excited to have long conversations with me. I was equally excited because I could learn a lot from her.

Her family had lived in a village in the Shaolin Temple valley for many generations but, in about 2010, when the Temple became a UNESCO World Heritage Site, the money-obsessed abbot decided that the village must be destroyed to make way for more tourist-oriented attractions. Everybody was kicked out and the village buildings were destroyed. It seems, however, that Sara's family were quite wealthy and although they had to move, they were allowed to keep their two very successful restaurants just on the edge of the Shaolin Temple grounds, and her grandfather and his family were permitted to live upstairs in one of them. As Sara was 'family', she and her friends were allowed into the Shaolin Temple grounds free of charge – which was very convenient for me.

One glorious autumn day, she took me up in the smaller cable car to see Huike's house again. There seemed to be some construction going on, but Sara took me straight to the little house and after making the requisite three bows at the entrance, she led me inside.

Huike's house

She told me that after Huike left, the local villagers took care of his house in honour of him, and generation after generation of villagers looked after it and made repairs when needed. Thus it was still standing. She showed me the roof and some walls at the back which she said were made of the same local materials from which the original house was built in order to preserve its authenticity as much as possible. I asked Sara what the current construction was all about and she asked some of the monks lazing around who told her that there were some rooms being built for monks who wanted a quiet place to live and meditate.

A few years later, during one of my last visits to China, I again went up to visit Huike's house, this time alone. From here, the views of the whole area were stunning because of the autumn colours everywhere. But to my horror, I saw that the little house had disappeared and there was now a big new ugly concrete building in its place.

I saw two American tourists who had an English-speaking monk as a tour guide so I asked the guide what had happened to the little house. He told me they had got rid of it and built this nice new place instead. I was devastated and asked him why they would destroy something of such historical significance, and his disturbing answer was 'Oh, it was too messy!'

I have noticed elsewhere that the Shaolin Temple authorities have, in their greed for the tourist big bucks, destroyed so much that is of real historical value. Buildings which in England would be preserved by various historical organisations are now often destroyed in modern China. My few photographs of Huike's little house are now all that remain of this precious glimpse of the history of the Zen Patriarchs.

Sengcan (also known as Sosan) (? – 606)

If little is known about Huike, even less is known about the Third Zen Patriarch, Sengcan – or Sosan, the Japanese form of the name. Possibly the four-year period, from 574 to 578, of political unrest and severe persecution of Buddhism and its spiritual leaders, was a reason for this. During this dangerous time Huike fled to some mountains to hide, and it was here that he transmitted the Dharma to Sengcan, who had become his disciple.

After receiving the transmission, Sengcan lived in hiding on Wangong Mountain in Yixian and then on Sikong Mountain in southwestern Anhui – the province next to Henan where Song Mountain is. Later, when it was safe to do so, it seems he wandered around central China, returning for a while, according to legend, to Mount Taishi in the Song Mountain range.

I knew of Sosan because Osho had spoken on his famous text called Xin Xin Ming (or Hsin Hsin Ming in Japanese). Osho's extraordinarily beautiful series of discourses were published as: 'Hsin Hsin Ming: The Book of Nothing'. In the book he says:

When a Sosan speaks, he speaks totally on a different plane. He is not interested in speaking; he is not interested in influencing anybody; he is not trying to convince you about some theory or philosophy or 'ism'. No, when he speaks his silence blooms. When he speaks, he is saying that which he has come to know and would like to share with you. It is not to convince you, remember – it is just to share with you.

And if you can understand a single word of his, you will feel a tremendous silence being released within you.

The picture of the following rather modern-looking house is a recent restoration of a very old, almost ruined, building high up on Mount Taishi. According to YaJun it seems that Sengcan did spend some time living on Mount Taishi, where the local villagers built the little house for him and took care of him. Apparently it is possible to visit the house – Yajun went there and took this photo and offered to take me if I wanted to go – but it would have meant a long steep hike up the mountain on little-known and uncared-for footpaths, and my ageing body was unable to manage this feat.

Once again I wished I had discovered Song Mountain and its intriguing heritage when I was a bit younger and more active!

Sengcan's house restored and maintained by local people

Daoxin (580 – 652)

It seems that Sengcan was quite a retiring kind of master, not given to much action. His successor, Daoxin, was very different.

After he became awakened, Daoxin moved to other areas of the country and set up the first exclusively Zen monastery at the foot of Broken Top Mountain in the province of

Hubei. The first three Patriarchs had preferred a life of relative solitude and insecurity – wandering here and there to teach their doctrines. Daoxin's idea was that it would be easier for people to go deeper into the ways of Zen if they lived and worked together, and so he set up the monastery. Here the Zen concept of working for your living (instead of begging or receiving donations) started – work became part of one's 'worship' – and the monastery became a commune with the monks engaging in all the work necessary to sustain their lives. In this way the concept that Zen should be more than just meditating for a few hours in a Hall but should extend to all aspects of one's daily life, arose. This became a central objective in Zen practice which still exists today.

Daoxin also added some popular Buddhist practices to Damo's pure Zen tradition, such as chanting the Heart Sutra. With these small changes, Zen was accepted by many more people and grew much more popular. Many came to visit Daoxin's monastery and were able to imbibe the flavour of Zen.

Hongren (602 – 674)

The Fifth Patriarch, Hongren, a disciple of Daoxin from whom he received the Dharma transmission, was an even stronger figure and his fame surpassed his master's. Because of him, Zen now became widely practised in China. He preferred the practice of cultivating awareness in daily life rather than incessantly studying and chanting ancient scriptures, which wasn't very popular. It is unlikely that he went to Song Mountain, the home of Zen. Instead, he moved south to Mount Pingmu, north of Guizhou Province, near Chongqing. Because of this, I have no personal connection with him or any little anecdotes to tell.

Huineng (636 – 713)

Huineng, the Sixth Zen Patriarch, almost overshadowed Bodhidharma. He lived from 636 to 713. His is an amazing story, although there are doubts about how much of it is true or how much is a fabrication by one of his supposed disciples. Huineng was interested in returning to Bodhidharma's original teachings -- most specifically the concept of 'instant enlightenment'.

Huineng's teachings were recorded by a disciple in a famous text called 'The Platform Sutra', two copies of which were found in the Library Cave in the famous Mogao Caves in Dunhuang, many miles away from where Huineng lived in southern China. (I asked a few scholarly Chinese friends how the documents had travelled so far but sadly didn't get any answers.)[3]

The two texts, which date from between 830 and 860, have been very important for the historical understanding of Zen. However, the sutras were probably written by a disciple because Huineng himself was, despite his brilliance, an uneducated and illiterate man unable to read any of the scriptures studied by other monks. He apparently became enlightened on just hearing The Diamond Sutra.

On one of my many visits to the Chuzu Temple on Song Mountain, I found an information board which explains – in frustratingly poor English – how Huineng had come there to pay homage to Bodhidharma. He brought a cypress tree to plant in Bodhidharma's honour; it is now about twenty feet high. There are many of these kinds of trees in the Song Mountain area. Zhongyue Miao has many. They grow very slowly but live to be thousands of years old. The famous tree in the Songyue Temple has been scientifically proved to be one of the oldest trees in the world – over 4500 years old.

Needless to say, I give Huineng's tree a hug whenever I visit the Chuzu Temple; my own way of paying my respects to Huineng – and indeed to all of the great Zen masters who have walked and meditated on Song Mountain.

Cypress tree planted by Huineng at the entrance to the Chuzu Temple, in honour of Bodhidharma

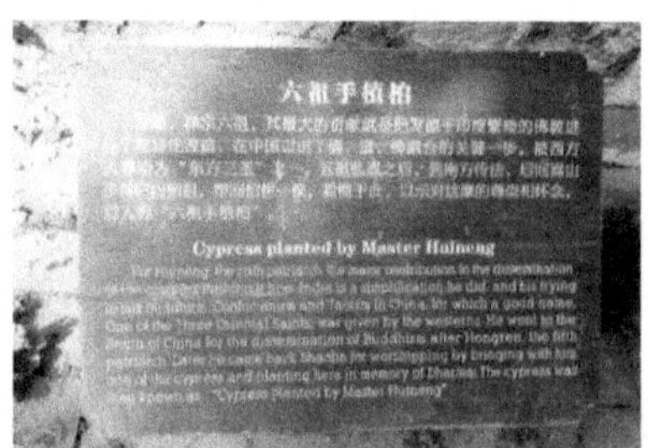

Information Board in the Chuzu Temple

From the little information I can find, it seems that, in the context of Zen, the definition for the word 'patriarch' is that a master has passed on the Dharma to his successor and presented him with a begging bowl and a robe as symbols of the transmission. There is no record of Huineng doing this. In fact, just before he died he supposedly told his disciples: *'You should act as though I were still in the world... After I die, just go on practising as before, as though I were still here.'*

In this way the lineage of the Zen Patriarchs ended.

6
A Trip to Yanshi

A painting of Xuanzang's hazardous journey from China to India in 629 AD

*What draws friends together
does not conform to the laws of nature.*

Jalal ad-Din Muhammad Rumi

A Trip to Yanshi

It has been said somewhere that the greatest mass migration of modern times is the annual journey home which millions of Chinese make to celebrate the Chinese New Year. Being with one's family is obligatory, so roads, trains, buses and planes – any conveyance that can be grabbed – are full to capacity with people rushing home.

Something similar occurs during the autumn National Holiday – from the 1st to 7th October – although admittedly not to such a large extent. And the purpose of this secondary movement of travellers is not to be with family, but rather to visit touristic or cultural sites, one of the most popular of which is the Shaolin Temple. If you happen to live on the twelve-kilometre-long road from Dengfeng to the Temple you face four or five days of total bedlam.

The road is four lanes wide and from 7am in the morning, police rearrange the lanes so that three are for outgoing traffic, and only one for incoming traffic, to allow all the vehicles – private cars, taxis and huge tourist coaches – to try to reach the Temple from the centre of town. At 4pm the arrangements are reversed to allow the tourists to return.

A twelve-kilometre all-day traffic jam is the result. No local buses, taxis or other vehicles are allowed to travel on the road during these four busy days.

The road cuts through the middle of Shilipu village, resulting in the usual peace and quiet being utterly shattered as frustrated, angry drivers turn off onto the two small roads leading into the village and race along them in the hope of finding another way forward and/or some public toilets. It is a vain hope – there aren't any, so you can imagine the consequences. They return to the main road even more frustrated and angry. What they are doing is highly dangerous because usually it is a sleepy village with almost no traffic to endanger the small children playing freely in the narrow streets, which are also full of young kungfu students from the small school next door to my house practising their kungfu forms, dogs lying around everywhere fast asleep, and old people chatting to their neighbours.

On one occasion, when I was dreading this imminent chaos which I found so hard to cope with, Ibo visited me just a few days before it was due to start. I told him of my concerns and was relieved to sense his fertile brain immediately ticking over with possible options. (I often called him an 'ideas-machine' because he was a classic example of someone who can think very quickly and creatively 'outside the box'.) Sure enough, in the evening, he called me to say that, as he too had a holiday, he had made arrangements to travel to a town called Yanshi, on the Luoyang side of the mountain, where he had booked a small out-of-the way hotel for us to stay in. There we would meet his friends, Mr Dong and Mr Duan, who had a car. Ibo assured me that no tourists would be heading in this direction. This was very good news and very thoughtful of him. He was such a good friend! To get there, we would take the local bus down the terrifying Song Mountain pass and then change to another bus to go to Yanshi. The local buses, I knew, were old, small and uncomfortable, but I didn't care – I just wanted out.

But driving through the Song Mountain pass is really a hair-raising ordeal. The narrow two-lane road cuts through rugged steep slopes with continuous curves and uneven, pot-holed, poorly-maintained surfaces. On the edge of each side of the road there is a four-foot-deep drainage channel which diverts the gushing waters of the heavy summer rains. So without a secure hard shoulder, the slightest driving misjudgement can easily lead to a rapid plunge into the ditch. And that would result in the mind-boggling chaos of having to get the vehicle out of the ditch, in the midst of traffic where you can't even pass another vehicle. And then there are the massive trucks which carry endless tons of stone and gravel from the huge quarries in the foothills of the mountain to the south. They are part of the constant frenzy of supply chains which feed the construction boom still taking place all over China. Many times I have held my breath as one of these huge trucks edged past the vehicle I was travelling in with just a few inches to spare. Even the empty returning trucks were so huge that they forced the oncoming traffic to screech to a halt on many of the curves in the road.

The reason this road is so neglected by the authorities is that there is now a recently-constructed highway to Luoyang, which runs south of this pass. However, these monster trucks are not allowed to travel on this new highway, and for local people travelling north and east, it is very inconvenient, and expensive because of the road tolls.

That day, however, the travel gods were (yet again) well and truly with me, because the day before we were due to leave, Ibo called me again to say that Mr Duan was very concerned that this poor old foreign lady would have to travel by dilapidated local bus, and had decided that he and Mr Dong would drive over the mountain to pick us up in Shilipu village. I was very touched. This was just one more example of the generosity that I have met over the years from so many Chinese people. They really do have very big hearts … over and over again I was to benefit from their genuine kindness and friendliness.

They must have made a very early start because at nine o'clock they were outside my house, having already picked Ibo up, blaring the horn impatiently from a comfortable new white SUV. My transport to Yanshi had been instantly upgraded from a shabby little local bus to a luxury vehicle! Both men were charming and Mr Duan immediately provided bottles of water and some tasty *baozi* in case we hadn't had breakfast. Being so early, the road wasn't yet very full with tourists visiting the Temple, so we made good time until we arrived at the peak of the mountain, just past the Temple, before descending via the treacherous pass on the other side to the Luoyang plains which led eventually to the Yellow River.

Then disaster struck. One of the dense fogs that the area is notorious for at this time of the year, suddenly descended on us and visibility was immediately reduced to less than a metre. I was now seriously nervous as I knew that, even with good visibility, the road was already dangerous, but with poor visibility it would be perilous. Luckily, Mr Duan saw a chance of tagging behind the same local bus which we had originally planned to travel on, and grabbed it. These bus drivers make the trip several times a day every day, in all weathers, and could do it blindfolded, so all Mr Duan had to do was stick close on the heels of the skilled bus driver in front who, unknowingly, managed to get us safely down to the foot of the pass.

Once we were on a much safer road, the ongoing fog was no longer a problem, and Ibo told me that they had arranged to visit the birthplace of an historical figure so important and so famous that even I had heard about him. His name is Xuanzang and he was a Buddhist monk, philosopher, translator – and most famous for his epic journey to India to study original Buddhist scriptures.

 Xuanzang was born in 602 in Chenhe Village in the district of Luozhou, the youngest of four children of a highly-educated and well-known family. He showed great intelligence and scholarship from an early age.

After the death of his father when he was nine years old, he made frequent visits to his older brother, Chengsu, who was an ordained Buddhist monk in a monastery in Luoyang, and started to study sacred Buddhist texts. He was allowed to take Buddhist orders when he was only thirteen years old.

Due to civil unrest, Xuanzang and his brother moved to the monastery of Kong Hui in Sichuan province where they continued to study Buddhist scriptures and where Xuanzang became a fully ordained monk at the age of twenty. He soon became deeply confused and frustrated by the many mistakes in the translated Buddhist texts currently available, so he decided to go to India to learn Sanskrit in order to study the original texts and learn from the great scholars and philosophers present there.

In 629 he set out on an epic journey across mountains and unknown desert areas with hostile inhabitants until he finally arrived at his destination: Nalanda, a prominent Buddhist monastic academy, located southwest of the modern city of Bihar in the northern Indian state of Bihar. Historians consider this academy to be the world's first residential university and one of the finest centres of learning in the ancient world. Xuanzang spent fourteen years there, learning Sanskrit and studying Buddhist philosophy and Indian metaphysics. Very quickly his reputation as a scholar became so great that even the powerful King Harsha, ruler of North India, wanted to meet and honour him. Enjoying this king's patronage, Xuanzang's return trip to China, begun in 643, was much easier.

Travelling back along the now much used Silk Road, he passed through the Buddhist centre in Dunhuang in Gansu province and eventually arrived back in Chang'an (now Xi'an), in Shaanxi province in 645, after an absence of sixteen years. He was welcomed as an honoured son and was offered many prestigious positions, but he declined them all and started on his great work of translating the many scriptures he had brought back from India. Xuanzang spent the remainder of his life translating these and other scriptures. His contribution to the study and practice of Buddhism in China and many other eastern countries, is immeasurable.

ॐ

Leaving the main road, we drove through the outskirts of a small town and entered what looked like an abandoned construction site. Looming through the still thick fog was a very large building with the typical temple roof. Ibo told me that we had now entered the grounds of a project started a few years before by a Buddhist nun who had decided that she wanted to build the biggest temple in China to honour Xuanzang. It would be called the Temple of the Ten Thousand Buddhas, decorated with ten thousand buddhas carved in jade. Very expensive!

Her grandiose schemes soon fell apart as her followers grew tired of her constant demand for money, her egotistical claims, and the realisation that actually the very revered White Horse Temple, birthplace of Buddhism, as well as the Longmen Caves (where I first saw a reference to the phrase 'The Ten Thousand Buddhas') were nearby, and people felt that these sacred places were of far greater significance than anything she could build. As far as I can discover, the project has been abandoned with the temple only half finished.

❧

Having parked the car we walked up to the huge temple, entered, and found towering scaffolding still in place and piles of decorative motifs and abandoned statues scattered everywhere. It really was bizarre. I could sense that both Mr Duan and Mr Dong were very disapproving of such a waste of effort and money and so we fortunately didn't linger but walked down a small hill into a charming village, full of trees, and finally ended up in front of the unpretentious family home of Xuanzang.

Here the atmosphere was very different. It seems the Chinese urge to modernise and Disneyfy everything had not yet reached this remote place and, according to Mr Duan, the house was more or less the same as it had been when Xuanzang lived there because, although he had left, the family continued to live there for generations and so kept the building in good repair. It was now lovingly cared for by a small Trust run by the local villagers, with government grants. Of course, some of it has been rebuilt but there is a genuine desire to maintain as much of the original structures as possible.

The only note of discord was an obviously modern wooden statue of a phoenix. I asked Ibo what the significance of this was. He said that the phoenix is the symbol of the feminine in China whereas the dragon is

Xuanzang's house

Mr Duan, Mr Dong and Ibo

A painting depicting Xuanzang's epic journey through challenging terrain on his way to India

the male symbol – so this phoenix statue had been put there as tribute to the nun who was doing such great things, probably by herself! Again I saw Mr Duan pull a face – it was easy for me to guess his opinion.

Ibo guided me to a well which, he said, had been there since the time of Xuanzang and had supposedly very pure and healthy water. As

Ibo drinking water from the ancient well

visitors were invited to drink the water, Ibo let the bucket down and pulled up some of the precious water for us to drink.

It was quiet and peaceful, with the fog adding an ethereal dimension of unreality, and I thoroughly enjoyed the visit. It was also a huge bonus to have Ibo there both to translate and also inform me about what we were seeing. So often visiting interesting places in China, I had only a minimal understanding of what I was seeing because of the lack of English, so this was a special treat.

❧❧

It was now well past lunch time so we drove further into Yanshi where Mr Duan took us to an unusual restaurant, run, apparently, by the community, and the excellent food was cooked by volunteer town people. It was buffet style and I was of course the centre of attention when I went to collect my food as, Ibo explained, foreigners were extremely rare in Yanshi. During the whole four days I was in the area I didn't see another non-Chinese person.

We then proceeded to the hotel Ibo had booked, just outside the town, and Mr Duan left us to settle in. I was happy to have a rest and I could see that Ibo was tired. His job was very stressful and his health, although better, was never good. In fact, as the days progressed, I began to see that the trip was also a bit of a medical visit for him. I will explain as I go along.

That evening we ate in the small restaurant in the hotel and I found out that Ibo and Mr Dong had enjoyed a refreshing hot tub and massage experience in the spa of the hotel which mostly served businessmen and their related conferences – there were no tourist sites nearby. It was good to see Ibo with restored energy. (Unfortunately, there was to be no such treat for me, as the hotel had no spa for ladies.)

The following morning Mr Duan arrived to pick us up and to take us into Yanshi for the ubiquitous, seemingly universal, millet-gruel breakfast. I did manage to find some hard-boiled eggs to eat with the

equally universal tasteless steamed bread. (Decent, wholemeal, multi-grain organic bread was one of the things I missed most when I was in China. In fact, on one of my journeys home, I took many photos of a wonderful bread shop in Frankfurt airport, complete with various delicious sandwiches, to send back to friends in China with a caption 'This is what real bread looks like.' I doubt if they were impressed.)

My feeling that our trip was a business-combined-with-pleasure one proved to be correct as it transpired that we were going to visit a well-known Chinese Traditional Medicine (TCM) doctor. I was so pleased as I have long been interested in Traditional Chinese Medicine and consider it to be the best medical system ever to be devised. I had had excellent treatment from two TCM practitioners in England and tried some remedies in China with amazing results. For example, for about two years I had been suffering with a very swollen and painful knee, making walking difficult. Despite various treatments from my doctor and consultants in the UK, nothing helped. Then on one visit to Beijing my young friend, Yujie, took me to a local TCM pharmacy where the doctor there recommended some healing 'patches' which I was to stick onto the knee. After only two weeks my knee was totally back to normal.

Ibo felt that Mr Dong had saved his life by treating him with a combination of traditional kungfu systems designed to confer optimum health on the body, and some Traditional Chinese Medicine medications. But Mr Dong openly declared himself to be an amateur in comparison to the man we were going to visit. Unfortunately I don't remember this doctor's name so I will, for convenience's sake, call him Mr Zhao. Although he looked like and acted with the energy of a man of twenty-five years old, I was very surprised to hear that Mr Zhao was in fact fifty-two.

He was famous in the area for his skills, and was rather unique in that he had trained in his youth with an old man who was the physician to the tragic Henry Puyi, the so-called 'Last Emperor', who died in Beijing in 1967. After his death, the physician moved to his home town of Yanshi and continued to practise and teach younger doctors, including Mr Zhao. What a heritage.

We arrived at an unprepossessing little shop, open to the street, and I was introduced to Mr Zhao who was an extremely cheerful individual and smiled all the time. I was absolutely fascinated. Here was 'old' China. The doctor was available for anybody to come into his little shop and be treated with herbs and acupuncture at a very low cost. The shop was full of cupboards with many drawers in which the herbs were stored. I watched when a patient arrived.

First Mr Zhao felt her pulses. In western medicine, we recognise one

Mr Zhao in his surgery which is open to the street so anybody can just walk in and be treated

pulse on the wrist: the heart beat in the radial artery. A good Chinese doctor, however, can recognise up to thirty-six different pulse qualities by touching the patient's wrist in various places to various depths. This ancient diagnostic art, along with other techniques, is often able to identify problems and pathologies well before they show up in the body, and it is still taught in TCM Colleges all over the world.

Once the diagnosis was made, Mr Zhao, with the help of his apparently very knowledgeable wife, accessed various drawers and pulled out different herbs which he measured onto a piece of newspaper. Ibo told me that the patient was then instructed to boil the herbs together in water for a certain time and drink the resulting potion. I already knew that the herbs were more powerful when prepared by this method

Work and socialising mix comfortably

than when taken in a powder form as is the modern, more convenient way.

The patient, a young woman, didn't seem at all surprised to be watched by four interested people – with Mr Zhao's son in the background watching a loud horror movie on the TV.

In between the constant stream of patients, there was obviously an intense discussion going on about Ibo's health and his pulses were duly read and medicine prescribed. I was relieved that there seemed to be no undue worry about his current condition. Ibo told me that he had also brought his mother to see Mr Zhao a few weeks previously. She was suffering from the onset of dementia but the medication she had received had already seemed to have halted the progression of the disease. And when I met her seven years later, she was fine, no sign of dementia. Ibo organised further medication for her which his brother would collect. His family lived in Gongyi, a small city only a few miles away.

It was such a friendly, relaxed meeting. It reminded me of the easy-going small shops in India where business life was mixed with the social visits of friends and family and frequent rounds of hot chai (tea). Here too, the lines between the private and the public, between work and family, were comfortably blurred.

Ibo told me that Mr Zhao could easily have a modern 'surgery' and charge huge prices for his skills and medication, but he didn't want this. He believed that as a doctor, it was his mission to help everybody, and money and prestige should never be an issue. Maybe this is why this lovely man never stopped smiling; in fact, he seemed quite buddha-like to me. I really felt privileged to meet him.

క్రాడ

But the Chinese never miss their meals so before long the wooden shutters were drawn across the shop opening and we walked to a nearby restaurant. That I was a vegetarian didn't seem to be an issue and it was a delicious meal – as is so often found in small family-run restaurants. Before we had left the shop, however, there seemed to be some verbal exchanges and Mr Zhao took out a short wooden ladder and climbed up to a top drawer where he took out something which he wrapped in a bit of newspaper and put in his pocket.

After the cheerful and delicious meal, some glasses, a teapot and hot water were brought, and Mr Zhao took out the small object he had wrapped in newspaper and proceeded to shave it with a penknife into a teapot with hot water. The object looked like a dried root or stem, about two cms long and one cm wide. Everyone was given a small glass of this special tea but fortunately I asked for only half a cup!

By mid-afternoon the party broke up and Mr Zhao returned to his shop and Mr Duan took us back to the hotel for a rest and, I imagined, more spa treatment for Ibo and Mr Dong. By the time we got back to our rooms I was ready to lie down because I wasn't feeling very well – and within an hour I was violently sick. Fortunately there was a western-style toilet in the attached bathroom, rather than the usual squat one, because I was doomed to spend a great deal of the night sitting on it. When Ibo came in at about 6 pm to take me out for the evening meal I was prostrate on the bed, feeling like death. I asked him what on earth was in that tea but he didn't know the English word and had to check it in his phone dictionary: rhubarb! I told him that in the west we consider that rhubarb leaves are toxic for the body but Ibo said the Chinese considered it to be a cleanser. It is possible that the rhubarb had been mixed with something else but I wasn't about to investigate – I just knew I was having an extreme reaction to it.

Ibo called Mr Dong who thought about calling Mr Zhao and asking for help but, remembering India again, and the very many times I had suffered similar such bouts of illness, I asked them please to go and get me some bananas. In China almost no milk is used in the diet, and no curd or yoghurt at all, so my usual Indian panacea for this kind of attack – bananas and yogurt – was not available. But still, bananas might help. The two men hurried off and apparently found a taxi to take them to a shop where they bought some bananas – three dozen of them! The ever-generous Chinese at work again! Perhaps the bananas did the trick because the next morning I felt better but just wanted to rest in the hotel room. I told Ibo and Mr Dong there was no need for them to stay, so they were gone for most of the day, but Ibo called me at regular intervals to check up on me.

By the evening I was completely recovered, so Mr Duan came to take us out for a meal. During our dumpling supper Ibo told me that they had planned that day to take me to the burial place of Du Fu, considered to be the greatest poet in Chinese literature. I knew about him because I had once noticed a book of his poems in Ibo's room and I naturally asked about him. Du Fu was born in Gongyi, Ibo's home town, in 712, and died in 770. The tomb, Ibo told me, is quite basic and not many people visit it as it is far from anywhere, but there are extensive grounds filled with many plants and trees so it is a lovely quiet place to wander in. I was of course very sorry to have missed this little expedition.

જી⊸ર્જી

We checked out of the hotel early the next morning as apparently we had an important visit to pay that day before going back to Shilipu and Dengfeng. We took a taxi into Yanshi where we met Mr Duan, who was already having breakfast in a street café. Ibo, noticing my face, went off without a word and returned soon after with a much-appreciated bag of *baozi* for me. Very thoughtful of him.

Amidst the noisy slurps of the gruel (another reason why it's not my favourite breakfast) Ibo told me that they were going to visit another Traditional Chinese Medicine doctor; in fact, the man to whom Ibo had gone for treatment three years previously when he had been so seriously ill with his liver complaint. He had stayed there for treatment for three weeks but became very depressed and felt that he was getting worse, so he left the place and returned to the huge hospital in Zhengzhou where he had been treated before.[4]

Looking fixedly at his gruel Ibo nonchalantly said, 'But first we have to pick up the prostitute.' I was used to being teased often by him but this one stopped me dead. He then looked at me and the smile hovered… 'OK,' I said, 'explain!' It seemed that Mr Duan had a girlfriend on the side – I would have used the word 'mistress' rather than 'prostitute'– but I could see that the latter word had far more interest and dramatic impact for Ibo. She was going to join that day's expedition. We duly picked up a rather flamboyant young woman with bright red hair but she was bubbly and full of fun and I could see why Mr Duan favoured her company. She had never met a westerner before and she was fascinated by me and kept touching my hair and the blonde hairs on my arm. Ibo said she asked him how I got my hair that colour.

৵৽৵

We soon left the main road and drove deeper and deeper into a country area. I got a weird feeling that I was going back in time. The countryside was untouched by modern life except for the odd car. It was beautiful and strange at the same time. We headed directly towards the Song Mountain range of mountains but it was a view I had never seen before. Houses and dwellings became fewer and further apart and after one last beautiful vista of big trees which reminded me of a Constable landscape, the terrain became sparse – empty except for an occasional farmer in the distant fields spread out around us. The road became a dirt track.

Quite close to the foothills of the mountain we entered an enclave through a discreet entrance partially hidden by bushes which opened onto a bare piece of land with a few isolated buildings on it. Two of them were small temples and the third was the office of the doctor. In contrast to the cheerful Mr Zhao, who we had met in Yanshi, this doctor was dour and serious and I could see why Ibo did not easily get along with him. However, another intense medical discussion ensued with Ibo being checked over thoroughly and a fairly positive verdict seemed to be reached.

I and the lady friend wandered around outside in what I felt to be a rather eerie place. Then Ibo emerged, beckoned to me and told me he wanted to show me where he had stayed in his difficult time there; he also had a surprise for me, he promised. He led us back the way we

had come and then, through a narrow opening in the hedge, showed me a steep flight of stone stairs leading to a hidden area, a kind of cleft in the hillside.

There was nothing surprising here but Ibo led me further to another set of stone steps into another dip, with cave dwellings leading off from it. This was extremely strange. I could see why he would feel oppressed being here, especially if he was ill. But he was still intent on showing me something else and led me into a small cave with some kind of basic stone furniture… And then into another. And another.

He started to tell me the disturbing story of this place. During the Chinese Cultural Revolution (1966 -1976), the aim was to preserve communism by purging the party of 'the four olds' (Old Ideas, Old Culture, Old Habits, and Old Customs), which meant getting rid of any traditional, intellectual or cultural leaders and organisations. Numerous

party officials, scholars, artists, gifted intellectuals, as well as religious leaders and their followers, were humiliated and ousted from their positions. They were often sent to very remote areas of the country where they could not form any kind of resistance groups. Many hundreds of thousands more were simply murdered.

A secret but strong underground movement developed which tried to help well-known figures in danger of being killed, by hiding and feeding them.

We were now standing in one such hiding place. Ibo told me that the doctor's parents, educated and intelligent, were very much involved in the underground movement in this area, and escaping intellectuals and political figures were hidden in these caves throughout the revolution. So remote was this place that they were never discovered and many valuable lives were saved.

Now the entrances to the caves were obvious but Ibo said that at that time this place was allowed to be overgrown with bushes and trees which effectively hid the entrances. The interiors of each cave were different, yet all contained some kind of stone 'furniture' for the unfortunate people to use. Some of the caves now housed statues of what looked like religious figures – I presume to be worshipped in some way. China has a strong tradition of using caves as both temples and dwellings. Ibo said that the caves even had tunnels behind them so that, in the event of discovery, the people could disappear into these tunnels and hide until the danger had passed.

The whole experience was a sobering one. I had of course heard often of the atrocities committed at this time all over China, but this particular place brought home to me the savagery of the revolution from which China has only recently started to recover.

Cave with stone 'furniture'

Cave now housing religious figures

As it was now lunchtime, the doctor invited us all to a simple lunch after which we set off on our return journey.

It seemed, however, that Mr Duan was enjoying the drive – and was apparently intent on showing me such very different aspects of the area – so instead of heading back to the main road, he continued to drive down the small dirt tracks weaving their ways through ancient farm lands, barely touched by modern times. It was silent and beautiful because the mountain range provided a constant arresting and atmospheric backdrop. I could feel its primordial power pervading our souls as we drove.

And it was somewhere during this drive that I had an extraordinary experience.

Gazing at the landscape it was as if a window opened in my brain, or my being, for a few seconds and I suddenly knew, without any shadow of doubt, that it was exactly around here that Osho had walked with Bodhidharma for three months. In his book, 'The New Dawn' Ch 23, Osho described how, in a past life, he had visited the Shaolin Temple on his way to Luoyang when Bodhidharma was meditating in the cave on Wuru Peak. Later, in another book: 'Glimpses of a Golden Childhood' Ch 6, he says: *I knew Bodhidharma personally. I travelled with him for about three months.* Remembering those words, I suddenly, inexplicably, 'knew' that this was one of the places on his short but highly significant journey with the great Damo.

The whole area has a unique ambience. Ancient texts tell us that after spending the nine years in a cave on Song Mountain and then introducing Zen to the people there, Bodhidharma crossed the mountain into this area which is the cradle of China's spiritual heritage. Between Yanshi and Luoyang, lies the revered White Horse Temple, built in 68 AD to house the first Buddhist monks coming to China from India. Nearby, the Longmen Caves in Luoyang, which would have been newly built at that time, were a definite homage to Buddhism.

A place untouched by modern China

Slightly to the west, on the road between Luoyang and Sanmenxia, near the village of Baibu, once stood a monastery where Bodhidharma lived and where his tomb (rebuilt in the fourteenth century) stands today.

Filled with the import of the surprising revelation I had just experienced, I felt blissfuly removed from the realities of the journey and only realised we were back on the mountain pass when Ibo spoke to me. He told me to get my camera ready and explained that there was one point from this road where we could get a brief glimpse of the old mountain pass down which many people of importance – LaoTzu, Bodhidharma, Osho (in a previous life), emperors and empresses (Wu Zetian), and so many other pilgrims and seekers – would have travelled. It was only a glimpse, but it was extraordinary to know that this very ancient and much-trodden pathway still existed today.

A slight indentation in the side of the mountain shows the ancient pathway leading down to the Luoyang plains from where we had just come

A few years later I asked YaJun for information about this pass and he sent me this old photo showing a strategic entrance in the ancient wall around Dengfeng which could be well-defended in the event of an attack from an enemy trying to approach via the old mountain pass.

Driving past the Shaolin Temple on our right, I saw to my relief that the hordes of visitors had nearly vanished and I knew that within one or two days the peaceful mellowness of our little village would be restored. Reaching my house, I profusely thanked the very generous Mr Duan, Mr Dong, Ibo, and the lady friend for what had been a remarkable four days. It had been a privilege and a pleasure to be with them and share their lives for a short time.

Back in my room, sitting quietly on my bed which faced my silently omnipresent mountain, I meditated both on the generosity of my Chinese friends, and on the very extraordinary revelation which I had experienced that day. Once again, I felt truly grateful that I had somehow found my way to this treasured place.

7
XinYiBa

Master Wu Nanfang in the Shaolin Temple

Sekkyo said to one of his monks:
'Can you get hold of emptiness?'

'I'll try,' said the monk,
and he cupped his hands in the air.

'That's not very good,' said Sekkyo,
'you haven't got anything there.'
'Well, master,' said the monk,
'please show me the way.'

Whereupon Sekkyo seized the monk's nose
And gave it a great yank.

'Ouch!' yelled the monk. 'You hurt me!'

'That's the way to get hold of emptiness,'
said Sekkyo

XinYiBa

There can't be many people less suited than me to be interested in kungfu. I have had a life-long aversion to any kind of sport. Yet here I was on a mountain in China becoming immersed in a little-known style of traditional kungfu – now called Gulun Kungfu – and, even more surprising, writing about it and becoming a kind of spokesperson for it! I have to smile at such incongruity.

As I have mentioned before, it was seeing the BBC documentary that brought me to this place, but it was also the character of Master Wu Nanfang and the meditativeness of his kungfu that impressed me. Master Wu Nanfang is a simple village man but his love and perception of Zen is deep, and I genuinely see his Gulun Kungfu as a manifestation of Zen in movement.

When I first met Master Wu Nanfang and his students in the village of Shilipu on the road between Dengfeng and the Shaolin Temple, the name used for his kungfu was ChanWuYi. Chan means Zen or meditation; Wu means the form or movement of kungfu; Yi means medicine or ensuring a healthy body using various means such as understanding the needs of the body, eating the right kind of food and, if needed, using traditional medicine and methods to heal. But even the three western men who were training at the school at the time couldn't say much more than that. They admitted that they were rather frustrated at not knowing more.

Enter my very dear friend, Yujie. She was a petite young woman who had come to visit her cousin, Rende – a star kungfu student whom I had recognised from his role in the documentary. He was fascinating to watch because all his movements were pure liquid – he didn't appear to have a bone in his body. He proudly brought Yujie to me to be introduced and I was happily surprised to suddenly be conversing in excellent English. She had an MA in English and worked as an English teacher in Beijing. Finally I could get some information about everything that was going on around me.

Yujie and Rende

I and the western students gathered around her to ask questions and **my** teacher's brain started to think that maybe we could get some more information about ChanWuYi if she would be willing to translate for us.

I would be very happy to help out by writing it all down in good English – I had a notebook computer with me and thought that we could get something printed out using a memory stick in one of the little computer shops in town. (This was before most people had personal computers or printers or WIFI etc. China hadn't yet jumped onto that technological bandwagon.)

Yuji quickly agreed to my proposal and with Rende we went to talk to Master Wu Nanfang to ask if he would be willing to talk about ChanWuYi and have his words translated. He was surprised – it had obviously not occurred to him that this would be useful – but he agreed and a meeting was set up for that afternoon. I asked Ibo to come too because, although his English was still at a basic level, my teacher's instincts recognised both an unusually high intelligence and a very natural ability to learn English quickly.

To be honest, the session wasn't easy. Master Wu Nanfang, or Shifu, as he was more commonly addressed as (Shifu means a kungfu teacher in Chinese) didn't seem to realise he should pause between sentences to allow Yujie time to write everything down, so I could see her getting frustrated. Also most of the concepts and terms were unknown to her so she struggled. I asked Ibo to write down as much as he could as well, and then, when Shifu stopped, I suggested that Yujie, Rende and Ibo come to my house so they could consolidate what they had each written down and translate a little bit to give me some clues.

This actually worked out very well (what a joy it was to be doing this with three such incredibly intelligent young people) and after another session with Shifu and another meeting at my house I felt I could begin to write something that made a bit of sense. Yujie read it back and enlarged on various points and, once I had made some corrections, I took my notebook down to the school and had a conference with the three western guys there, one of whom spoke good English. They were excited at the idea of finally learning some details of this kungfu and with their input I made even more alterations and went over it again with Yujie until we felt we had nailed it.

Ibo then took me and a memory stick into town to a small computer shop and we made a few copies of the four pages I had written.

Thus began my career as a Gulun Kungfu PR person.

෧෩

As the days passed, I learned more about the kungfu, especially from Ibo with whom I and two other people shared a flat. His command of English progressed rapidly. I learned about the physical qualities of this style of kungfu and really began to appreciate it for its profound scientific understanding of the human body and how to maintain optimal health.

I found out that Shifu loved Bodhidharma deeply and that, while most kungfu schools paid homage to Buddha, on Shifu's shrine in both his old and, later, his new school, was an image of Bodhidharma. His kungfu really did have Zen as an underlying concept – a 'spiritual dimension' if you like. But Shifu was also adamant that Zen should be part of one's everyday life and that that special awareness should be there twenty-four hours of the day; in other words, the aim was to be in a state of meditation all the time. Something I was also aspiring to.

In fact, one related lesson I really learned – the hard way – was to be 'in the present moment'. I had never lived closely amongst unsophisticated but intelligent people and I soon started to notice that my western conditioning of forever planning for the future or remembering the past was coming up against what I first thought was a kind of obtuseness, maybe even stupidity. But, watching myself, I slowly began to realise that when I – and other western students – brought our hyper-active western minds to a situation, Shifu simply smiled and calmly shrugged his shoulders as if to say: 'Everything will take care of itself. There is no need to worry or plan for the future because how do you know what will happen?' With Lijuan, I played some part in organising the arrival of foreign students so was of course intent on being efficient so that nothing went wrong. I had to really watch my irritation and, indeed, a feeling of helplessness, when she also sweetly shrugged off my attempts to be organised.

And I started to see that everything happened when it was supposed to happen and there was never a mishap. This was such a valuable lesson for me because it was so relaxing. Somehow their life had a rhythm and a trust to it whereby things just happened in their own time and with no fuss, even if we were dealing with foreigners arriving on planes from all over the world. For example, one young Australian man arrived at the airport but had forgotten to give us his flight number. Although Wenju went to pick him up in Zhengzhou, he couldn't find him. I got into a panic wondering how on earth this young man, only twenty years old, would manage to find this small school up the side of a mountain, but Lijuan just told me not to worry and everything would be all right. Sure enough, the young student eventually arrived, smiling broadly at the adventure of having been befriended by a Chinese family who could speak no English but were sufficiently intrigued to play detectives and discover the destination of the young man and deliver him safely. They were justifiably proud of themselves and were invited by Shifu to dinner as a reward.

Gradually the people living around Song Mountain helped me to understand a different reality – one without stress and worry and endless mind activity; one where all fuss and bother just naturally dropped away and a simple, peaceful being in the present moment took its place. And I recalled Osho's words:

Zen lives in the present.
The whole teaching is how to be in the present –

how to get out of the past which is no more
and how not to get involved in the future which is not yet,
and just to be rooted, centred, in that which is.
The whole approach of Zen is of immediacy,
but because of that it can bridge the past and the future.
It can bridge many things: it can bridge the past and the future,
it can bridge the East and the West, it can bridge body and soul…
It can bridge the unbridgeable worlds,
this world and that, the mundane and the sacred.

༄༅

My visits to China followed a pattern: I was there in the spring for two months – March and April – and in the autumn for nearly three months – from mid-September to mid-December. The rest of the year was either too hot or too cold for me.

On my next return to China six months later, I found that much had changed. To begin with, Shifu had had a huge board printed – about ten feet wide and eight feet deep – with a long quote about ChanWuYi in English, printed on it. This sign had attracted the attention of a number of westerners in Dengfeng who were studying kungfu, and they had decided to leave their current schools and come and train at this one. There were now eight foreign students there. Ibo's English had improved dramatically and he was now the manager of the foreign students and did a lot of other things as well, especially dealing with local council and provincial administrative matters. He was the only person there with any kind of higher education.

Ibo gave me almost no time to arrive before telling me he wanted to make a website and that he wanted my help. I had done a bit of work on websites in the UK so I thought this would be an interesting challenge and said yes. Ibo had found a small company in Zhengzhou (the nearby huge city) so one day we got on the bus with Lijuan and went to Zhengzhou to discuss things with this small company. They were very interested in this unusual – for them – project, but not one of them spoke English so I wondered how this would all work out. We got over this problem by them deciding that they could design the structure and then give us a small program so that we could add the necessary texts and photo ourselves They created a very attractive website and we added loads of lovely photographs and texts in English – prompted by Ibo of course – and as a result, more foreign students started to come. The word was out.

༚

By 2013 Master Wu Nanfang had achieved his heart's desire and bought a small piece of land with an old farmhouse – destined to be dismantled – in a protected National Park area on the opposite side of the valley, on Mount Taishi. It was an absolutely stunning position with unobstructed views over Mount Shaoshi. And now I really got to appreciate Shifu's sense of aesthetics because he designed and executed the new school building himself very beautifully – and also engaged all the students to help while instructing them to work with awareness of what they were doing.

Ibo had left to work with a local company who wanted an English-speaking person to liaise with two European companies to build some leisure activities on another part of the mountain. And the school had a new manager called Wenzhe, a talented and capable young man, well-educated, but one who I didn't particularly get along with. He was ambitious and wanted the school to grow but he saw foreigners as a means to get a much larger income – rather than considering them as individuals who had come a long way to train here.

After the Dengfeng area became a UNESCO World Heritage Site in

2010, it quickly turned into a popular tourist area and the charming, innocent, rural area I had fallen so much in love started to disappear quickly as the almighty bucks – or in this case, yuan – started to speak more and more loudly, started to scream, in fact. The kungfu schools jumped on the bandwagon as quickly as they could and targeted foreign students from whom they could demand high fees. Wenzhe thought the same way, although he was held in check by myself as well as Shifu, who was not much interested in money. He appreciated that foreign students came from so far away and made such great efforts to learn his beloved kungfu. Seeds of conflict were being sown.

Wenzhe asked me to help him make a much more sophisticated website, with him doing the Chinese section and me the English part. But he had very fixed Chinese ideas about the website and I quickly saw that they wouldn't work for an English website. But he wanted everything his way! In the end I managed a compromise that western people would understand and be attracted by – but it was neither easy nor fun. I missed Ibo's intelligence, his understanding of westerners and his wonderful humour.

Until now I had not really encountered the rigidity or narrow-mindedness of communism amongst the people I had met. The villagers and local kungfu practitioners were quite innocent and more or less did their own thing, being too remote to be affected by the powers-that-be in Beijing. And Yujie and Ibo were far too intelligent to allow their minds to be affected by communist party lines. But Wenzhe was very much a communist, and so we clashed. Shifu and his family did not pay obeisance to Mao Zedong, but Wenzhe practically worshipped him as a god. I remember him praising Mao as one of the great leaders of China, even of the world, and I asked him how he could reconcile that apparent status with the fact that he instigated the horrifyingly destructive Cultural Revolution and the disastrous 'Great Leap Forward', causing about thirty to sixty million people to die from starvation, malnutrition, or simply by being murdered. I had met one man who told me that his mother had made soup from tree twigs and leaves just so her children would have something warm and theoretically filling in their bellies. Wenzhe's reply was that the people loved Mao so much they were happy to die for him. I was appalled at this idiocy.

However, after a lot of hard work, the website was eventually ready to launch and the English part at least looked quite good.

Once this was complete, Wenzhe then had another project he wanted me to work on – a book about Gulun Kungfu! This would take a lot of time and effort and I wasn't keen. Although I of course wanted to help the school in whatever way I could, as well as the many western students who were enjoying the training and being in the rarefied ambience of the stunning Song Mountain, I felt that I wanted some time for myself to meditate and enjoy my limited time on the mountain, and not to have to work all day every day.

Fortunately help came with the arrival of a young western woman who fell in love with Wenzhe and together they wrote a lot of the book during the six months I was back in England. When I returned to China, I edited the book, consulting with an advanced kungfu student from the UK who knew a lot about kungfu and getting his feedback and approval on many points about which I was doubtful. As I had done with my other three books, I designed this book with the Kindle Direct Publishing template and published it on Amazon. It has sold very successfully around the world and attracted many students to come to the school.

But there was one part I wasn't happy about: I felt that the mysterious concept called XinYiBa – much bandied around by western kungfu students – had been wrongly explained in the book and I wanted to do something about it because I didn't want people to be misled. However, I could do nothing as there was nobody who had sufficient language skills to help me talk to Shifu, translate effectively, and get a clear explanation from him. From my point of view, he was the only person who really knew what XinYiBa was and therefore he was the only person who could explain it correctly.

꩜

Over the years I had helped Lijuan with answering emails from prospective students, many of whom spoke only basic English themselves and it took some detective work to figure out what they were saying. For Lijuan this was understandably difficult.

And after a while I noticed that, as often as every week, there was a person who said he was coming to China for four weeks to study XinYiBa. Somehow westerners had heard about this subject and seemed to think it was the next step in their study of kungfu. It now had a kind of 'cult status'. And they expected to learn it in four weeks! How could Lijuan explain that their expectations were totally unrealistic? It was so obvious that they had absolutely no idea what XinYiBa actually was. They had simply heard about it and wanted it – in four weeks, the length of the usual Chinese visa.

But it was a problem for the school because foreign students came with their unrealistic expectations and then got angry because they weren't being taught what they wanted. There had been quite a few unpleasant incidents with students because of this. But although I had an idea about what XinYiBa might be, I certainly had no obvious answers so I couldn't help with the situation.

꩜

One afternoon I sat outside under the overhanging roof of the school's Reception room and silently contemplated the softly falling rain veiling the mountain dimly visible in the distance. ChenGeng came and sat with me and in silence we watched the rain.

Suddenly it occurred to me that maybe I had been asking the wrong question. Always I had asked: 'What is XinYiBa?' – and always I was met with blank looks and dead silence. Now I thought to phrase the question in a different way and I quietly asked ChenGeng, 'With XinYiBa, how do you feel?'

For the first time I didn't get the blank response. He thought for a while and then said one word, 'Empty.' Then he obviously thought he was giving me a wrong impression and qualified his answer with the words, 'But have full power.'

A perfect answer! Pure Zen!

ChenGeng meditating on the mountain

I felt that my intuitive, possible understanding of XinYiBa had been tentatively confirmed. After another few minutes, ChenGeng went on to try to explain further. He said that once he had had an experience when doing his practice of suddenly 'opening up' and feeling an energy so incredibly strong that he 'fell down'. This, he thought, was XinYiBa.

He didn't know how much his simple words meant to me. I really felt he had given me a glimpse which corroborated what I had learnt from Osho, whose Zen message was actually very simple: be empty and you will be filled with the love, energy and divine power of existence.

I also remembered the Japanese Zen saying which I quoted at the beginning of this book: 'The emptiness of the full moon reflects the Zen mind.'

Feeling that I now had a vague glimpse into the ultimate heart or soul of Gulun Kungfu, a few days later, in a quiet moment, I asked Lijuan my newly-phrased question: 'With XinYiBa, how do you feel?' Again the blank look was absent. She thought for a while and then pulling out her phone she typed something into the phone's dictionary. She then showed me the answer – one word: *satori*. I felt like another piece of the puzzle had fallen into place because this word certainly meant something to me. She didn't know that the word '*satori*' was not English but Japanese, but seemed pleased to see that I understood and was very satisfied with her answer.

The word '*satori*' roughly means 'an experience of the divine, of existence, of something greater than the self, of a state approaching enlightenment'. Once a person experiences this state he is transformed forever; he can never go back to what he was before, because he has had a glimpse of something of the beyond. With this he now knows something about where he comes from, where or who he is, and where he is going. *Satori* is not yet the complete liberation of enlightenment, but it is a sign that the person is now on the way. Sometimes the experience can be so strong it is frightening – as ChenGeng described. And, as always, this experience cannot be described in words, only hinted at.

I feel, therefore, that one should be careful of someone who says he knows what XinYiBa is and proceeds to tell you. Currently there are many online websites telling people what XinYiBa is and there are many Chinese kungfu teachers bragging that they know all about it, and if you just do their course and pay them lots of money, they will tell you. They have learnt that foreigners are very interested in XinYiBa, know nothing about it but are keen to know more, so unscrupulous people are cashing in on that desire and, as XinYiBa is basically indefinable, they are not likely to be caught out.

✺

In the spring of 2019, I was again visiting Song Mountain and at the kungfu school I found that Wenzhe had left and Shifu's son, Wenju, was now the manager.

Studying kungfu there for two months was a young man called DongDong. DongDong spoke very good English and he told me that Shifu had asked him to translate the Gulun Kungfu book to him and was fairly satisfied with everything – except the part about XinYiBa. (Although Shifu was consulted on every point by Wenzhe, I still felt the explanation about XinYiBa was misleading, remembering, however, that it **is** extremely difficult to explain, especially in English.) So I was very interested to hear DongDong's comments and asked Shifu if, with his help, we could now discuss things. Perhaps we could finally be able to explain XinYiBa in a better way, a way that was easier for western people to understand, since none of the Chinese explanations I had heard so far had made any sense to me or to any of the other foreign students.

Instead of trying to explain, Shifu asked **me** how I would explain XinYiBa. I was rather surprised, but gave him a bit of a discourse about how I felt a westerner could have a glimpse of what XinYiBa might be – knowing full well that only when one had the experience of it could one really know. At the end of my explanation Shifu said something to DongDong who then turned to me and said: 'Shifu says you have understood perfectly. Please explain XinYiBa in this way to western people.'

৯৩

This then is my explanation…

Throughout the history of mankind there have been certain enlightened individuals or masters who have devised systems to help their followers to understand and go deep into their own consciousness, to know themselves, and therefore to know the truth of existence or universal consciousness. Nearly all masters started with a sort of training of the body, because, in the beginning, this is where we are.

Please understand that what I am describing here is **very** simplistic. I am using a few examples just to try to illustrate the connection between kungfu and XinYiBa.

Exactly when Buddha lived is not clear but dates mentioned are between 600 and 500 BC. A meditation technique associated with Buddhism, said in fact to be devised by Buddha himself, is called *Vipassana*: watching the breath; watching the incoming breath; watching the gap; then watching the outgoing breath and again watching the gap before the next inhalation. On the surface this looks to be a simple technique. In practice it is quite difficult.

The next system we know of is yoga, developed by Patanjali (a Hindu) whose dates are also not clear – he could possibly have lived around 200 BC. Very briefly, one could say that the paths practised in Yoga – meaning 'union' in Sanskrit – lead to liberation, transforming the life and the very existence of the practitioner. The yoga exercises were all designed with scientific precision to purify the body, remove attachments to it and so reach a state of 'Universal Consciousness'.

Sufi Whirling is another physically active form of meditation. It is particularly associated with Rumi, the thirteenth century poet master who wrote beautiful mystical poetry in Persian. The concept behind it is that by whirling continuously for many hours, the energy of the body eventually becomes centred at what the Chinese call the *dantian* (equivalent to the Japanese *hara*), enabling the individual to become so empty that he opens up and is filled with universal consciousness. To increase the chance of this happening, the whirler always turns with his right palm upwards – to more easily receive the universal energy – and his left palm downwards – to ground the energy so it falls downwards. In this way the whirler channels energy from his right hand, through the *dantian* at his centre, and then down to the ground. This enhances the transmission of energy to purify his body and himself – a bit like a lightning rod.

Latihan is another physical meditation developed by the Indonesian Master, Bapak Muhammad Subuh Sumohadiwidjojo (1901 to 1987) who started the Subud movement. Latihan is also about opening, using no particular method. Usually the practitioner is standing, breathing softly and quietly, tuning in and starting to resonate with a universal energy which causes the body to move slowly and gently and to purify itself. It is more easily done in a group with other people who are practiced in this meditation, because their energy can help a newcomer's energy.

This technique is widely used throughout Indonesia and the rest of the world. J.G.Bennett, one of Gurdjieff's disciples, was very interested in this technique.

Then there are the active meditations developed by Osho within the last fifty years. Osho's insight is that twentieth and twenty-first century people are very different from those who lived in the past. Adversely affected by modern technology, stressful lifestyles, unhealthy food and materialism, they are not easily suited to simply sitting down quietly for long periods of meditation. Osho said that new techniques were needed for people in this current age, so he developed five techniques all based on the same principle: start with the body. Osho draws on older traditional techniques but 'repackages' them to suit a person living in the stressful twenty-first century.

Osho's most famous and most powerful technique is Dynamic Meditation; the other four active meditation techniques are: Nataraj, Nadabrahma, Kundalini and Gourishankar. I won't describe them in detail here except to say they all start with the body, aiming to reduce its tensions and harmonise the individual with a universal energy and hopefully enlightenment. Many of the techniques also use the *dantian* as an important point of centering and gathering energy.

Of course there are many other systems – chanting or singing mantras, the wild dancing of the Bauls in India, Gurdjieff Sacred movements etc – which I haven't touched on. It would need an entire book in itself to do justice to them all.

✿

I explained to Master Wu Nanfang that my understanding is that XinYiBa is the Chinese concept of enlightenment, attained by practising, with absolute totality and awareness the comprehensive training system of kungfu developed over many, many years at the Shaolin Temple.

XinYiBa is **not** the highest level of kungfu – as it is commonly described. Rather, it is the transformation of the individual into a state of consciousness beyond the physical level, beyond body, heart and mind. It is a state of absolute consciousness which has been arrived at by the use of physical tools, in this case kungfu movements. As such it is in line with the other systems of physical trainings leading to a spiritual state, which I have outlined above.

In fact, glimpses of a heightened level of consciousness – when a person is so totally focussed that he enters another level beyond body and mind – are not uncommon in our everyday world; for example, in a crisis or life-threatening situation. And it is a commonly documented fact that people doing long-distance running sometimes enter a state of euphoria which enables them to keep running when medically the body shouldn't be able to do so. The point is that when a person enters another level of consciousness – and there are many different forms and degrees of this – the body no longer follows the usual physical laws and an individual can perform seemingly impossible tasks that he would not be able otherwise to achieve. Performed with totality over a long period of time, and combined with a devoted spirituality, especially with the help of an enlightened Master, the result can be enlightenment or XinYiBa.

One example well-known to disciples of Osho was how Osho sat with them in discourses for two hours or more. He would sit down, cross his left leg over the right one, and then, after talking and leading people in meditation, he would get up and walk normally out of the Meditation Hall. Medical experts say this is impossible, because the blood flow would be stopped when holding such a position without moving for such a long time. Osho clearly explained the phenomenon and others like it, using the example of Nijinsky, who jumped to seemingly impossible heights for seemingly impossible lengths of time. This feat was constantly wondered at as being unattainable in normal circumstances. Osho explained that Nijinsky was so total in his dancing that he entered a state of meditation or heightened consciousness, and was thus able to perform unimaginable feats.

When I explained this to Shifu with DongDong translating, Shifu began nodding his head vigorously and said he totally agreed with my explanation.

XinYiBa is therefore not a secret or a mystery but it **is** very difficult to explain to a westerner – and even to modern Chinese students – who don't have the tradition of oriental martial arts or meditation in their upbringing. It is also not a series of exercises or forms which get more and more difficult as a student advances – another fallacy. No, mastering a series of exercises does not lead to XinYiBa; rather, it is the other way around: as one enters a state of harmony and awareness – a higher level of consciousness if you like – then one becomes more able to execute higher levels of forms. This cannot be learned in the space of three or four weeks.

Language is a huge barrier here. Firstly, western languages, having very little vocabulary for meditation or enlightenment, simply have never managed to comprehensively describe these states. A modern dictionary does not give an adequate translation so it is almost pointless using one. (Remember, when Lijuan tried to explain XinYiBa to me her dictionary gave a Japanese word, not an English one!) How is a Chinese person, whose English is probably fairly limited, going to explain, even if he wanted to?

The situation is very open to misunderstanding and exploitation.

꩜

To perhaps help with a greater understanding of XinYiBa, it might be useful to trace its history from ancient times.

Bodhidharma arrived at the Shaolin Temple from India in the early sixth century. At that time, the monks were already practising kungfu,

Master Wu Nanfang practising XinYiBa

XinYiBa on Song Mountain

but as sport or for protection and defence. Bodhidharma would have been familiar with Buddha's and Patanjali's systems of physical movement and meditation to help their disciples advance towards a higher consciousness.

He therefore introduced the dimension of meditation to the kungfu already being practised by the Shaolin monks. This was very successful and became a recognised procedure in 1592 when the twenty-sixth Abbott, WuYang ZhenDao, defined and compiled a training system, incorporating meditation and XinYiBa, into a system called YongHua Tang which became known throughout China. Many students and seekers came to learn this special training.

The tradition reached a peak in the latter part of the nineteenth century when the monk, Wu Gulun (Shifu's great-great-grandfather), attained XinYiBa and was revered as one of the greatest masters of kungfu. The times were troubled, however, and the Abbot of the Shaolin Temple instructed Master Wu Gulun to leave the Temple, hide himself and protect the precious heritage of YongHua Tang and XinYiBa. He should only return when peace had been restored and then coninue to pass on what he knew.

In 1928 the event that had been so feared by the Temple's monks occurred. A warlord called Shi Yousan set fire to the monastery, burning it for over forty days. An entire heritage was lost, many monks died, the rest dispersed.

Master Wu Gulun's son, Master Wu Shanlin, continued to teach his father's Shaolin heritage in secret, handing down the precious tradition of Gulun Kungfu and XinYiBa to his sons and eventually Master Wu Nanfang. He did teach for three years at the Shaolin Temple after the fire, but then left because he felt that the calibre of the monks now at the Temple was very low and he did not want to impart such a precious heritage to people who could not understand and would not appreciate the quality of the kungfu he was teaching.

Current Chinese kungfu masters acknowledge Master Wu Shanlin and claim their lineage stems from him. This is not the case – or it is a very diluted knowledge, barely reaching a basic level, and absolutely not XinYiBa – because Master Wu Shanlin returned to his village after just three years and continued to impart his knowledge to just a few chosen students there. Master Wu Nanfang lived and practised with him when he was a very small child – he was six years old when Wu Shanlin died.

☙

Shifu tells his students that when the first Gulun Kungfu movement is performed, he or she is doing XinYiBa. He is right in a sense. You have taken the first step on the journey. But it is a very long journey requiring total commitment, dedication and devotion. It is a journey that cannot be understood by the mind, especially the westerner's analytical mind. It can only be experienced. And it has to become part of everyday life – practising awareness in work, in play, in sleep...[5]

Shifu working in the fields with students

As you practise, you start to get glimpses of something deep and fulfilling; you start to touch inner spaces you have never touched before; you feel the stresses and tensions of your life receding and a purity, harmony and silent emptiness taking its place. Something takes over; you are no longer performing forms or exercises. You have started on the path to experiencing a state of consciousness, an understanding of existence – the state of XinYiBa, or enlightenment.

8
A Tradition Destroyed

The one-hundred-year-old wall painting in the Shaolin Temple
showing traditional kungfu forms

A Rebellious Spirit

Between your birth and your death
your dance should remain
a conscious solitary reaching to the stars –
alone, uncompromising, a rebellious spirit.
Unless you have a rebellious spirit,
you don't have a spirit at all.
There is no other kind of spirit available.

Osho

A Tradition Destroyed

The kungfu school was doing well. As a result of the new website, the Facebook page and the book, many western students had found their way to this rather remote place and were seriously training, fortunately without any ambitions to 'study' XinYiBa! There was a warm cheerful connection between the ten foreign students, from five different countries, who were there when I returned in the spring of 2019.

The number of Chinese students had also increased, due no doubt to the quite exciting new website with all its videos and also, possibly, due to a very good documentary about the school, the training and Master Wu Nanfang – who was now a bit of a celebrity – made by one of the main Chinese channels, CCTV4, which had been filming there earlier in the year. [5]

With a considerable increase in the number of Chinese students, Shifu had rented a big house in Shilipu village (where I would later stay for a while). The senior students now lived there while the smaller boys and the foreign students stayed at the school.

The feeling was one of optimism and it was obvious that the family was enjoying not having to struggle financially as they had done for so many years. I was happy to see this because I knew very well that Shifu, being the only male in a family of five children, was expected to always support the extended family, in various ways and to various degrees, as well as his own.

Dongzhe, Wenju's wife, was now pregnant with her second child and we all loved seeing their first daughter, three-year old Zeyuan, trying out a few kungfu moves. There was no shortage of small teachers showing her what to do, although most of the training seemed to consist

The Wu family and friends in front of the kungfu school

of rolling on the ground and shrieking with laughter. Lijuan's eighteen-month-old baby boy was just gorgeous – now babbling away and very happy to entertain anybody who would pass the time of day with him in baby-speak.

The latest addition to the family ranks was Dongzhe's strikingly beautiful mother, Xiaohong, who had come to live at the school to take care of Zeyuan sometimes and also to look after some of the very little students who often, it was obvious, missed their mothers. Some of them were sent to the school when they were five or six years old. Xiaohong took everything in her stride and was fearless at trying anything new. We called her 'the wonder-woman' because she had done a lot of cycling in various parts of China on her own, and had recently ridden to Tibet and back in six weeks. She was so capable that she was even allowed to drive the precious big Honda 4 x 4 which was Wenju's pride and joy.

She was also, I learnt later, supporting her old parents whose house had one day, with no warning at all, collapsed and sunk into a hole which suddenly appeared when the ground terrifyingly caved in, pos-

Xiaohong and her old parents in their very poor house

sibly into an old mining excavation. They were forced to return to their former 'house' which was really a cheap pre-fab one-room shell with no comforts except fortunately some electricity, and running water from an outside tap. The toilet was an outside hole-in-the-ground and there was no shower. This building was freezing cold and the broken windows were stuffed with rags. I visited them there once and Xiaohong also took me past the site of their 'new' house which had vanished into the ground. It was eerie to see the site. I was enraged to hear that the old couple had received no compensation for the collapse of their small house.

The gap between those who had and those who hadn't was widening rapidly in modern China.

⊱⊰

One morning, walking up to the school, I met Xiaohong driving the big Honda with Shifu's wife, another friend and Zeyuan on board. Xiaohong stopped to say hello. Despite her lack of English, she was very expressive and energetic and while pointing vigorously to the mountain, kept repeating the words: 'BaiYouGou' which she knew I would understand.

BaiYouGou was the Wu family's ancestral village where two hundred years before, Master Wu Gulun went to live when he was told to leave the Shaolin Temple and live in secret to protect the Shaolin heritage until such time as it was safe to practise it openly again. The Wu family had lived in this hidden village since then. I had been there a few times before and been shown the family home – which I loved. It was like immediately stepping back in time because it seemed that the village hadn't changed for centuries.

Xiaohong knew my feelings so she jumped out of the car, saying one of the few English phrases she knew: 'Come-on! Come-on! ' and opened the passenger door, lifting Zeyuan out and indicating that I climb in. Zeyuan was repositioned on my lap. I was happy to go with them. But when we arrived at the village, we unexpectedly drove straight past it

BaiYouGou Village

further into the mountains, eventually hitting a dirt track that wove its way through thick bushes and trees, with the mountains looming on all sides, until we finally arrived at another very small village, very dilapidated. It was like a magical mystery tour for me as I had no idea what was going on but it was fascinating anyway. We were greeted with an assortment of people, one of whom, Xiaohong grabbed and said to me: 'mama' and pointed to Shifu's wife. I had vaguely heard that Shifu had married a woman from a nearby village so I assumed this was her family and we were visiting her family's home.

It was a very poor place but it had a certain charm. And it was bustling with energy! Somebody took my arm – the Chinese are very tactile and not at all shy – and proudly showed me some paper pictures of clothes, cars, houses and yuan. I quickly realised that this was probably a family funeral celebration because on other occasions I had seen these kinds of pictures being used to burn at the site of a family ancestor's grave as offerings to the departed family member. My understanding was confirmed when Xiaohong showed me some words on her phone dictionary which said 'ancestral worship'.

It transpired that Shifu's wife and her family were going to do the appropriate rituals at an ancestor's grave nearby, and in the meantime two other village women were preparing what looked like a big celebration feast for the midday meal.

Xiaohong had obviously been there before and seemed to be excited to show me something interesting. I had seen that this was obviously a cave dwelling (used extensively all over China in bygone days) and sure enough she led me into the kitchen which had been cut out of the hill side. She proceeded to guide me, with a flashlight, through rooms and tunnels which got progressively darker – a regular rabbit's warren of passages and caves. We must have been burrowing quite deep into the hill because it was cold and dark and I wasn't at all sure what I was supposed to see. But I took a few photos of the dark caves, after which I was led out into the sunlight and out to the entrance of the house where Xiaohong proudly showed me some Chinese words painted onto a kind of sign. After showing me the word 'soldier' on her phone she then did a great acting job of somebody shooting, other people being very afraid

Kitchen built into the mountain showing the entrance to a hidden passage at the back

and then scurrying into the house and the caves behind the obvious rooms. It seemed she was indicating that maybe some people had hidden in the caves from some soldiers.

When the family returned from their ancestral ceremony, other villagers arrived and we had a delicious lunch before returning home.

Back at the school I looked around for Michael and eventually found him having a nap. At my request for his translating expertise, he was of course happy to talk to Xiaohong. It seems that the village house had been commemorated by local authorities for saving many lives during

Caves cut deep into the mountain to save the villagers' lives

the Japanese invasion of China. Japanese soldiers managed to get this far inland, killing as many people as possible along the way, but when they arrived at BaiYouGou they found it deserted – and so left without doing any damage. Apparently the villagers had arranged a system of look-outs who were able to send word to the villagers when the Japanese were nearby, thus enabling the people to silently fade away onto hidden paths which ended up in Shifu's wife's family house. They hid deep in the caves where they had stored food and water. Not a single life was lost.

This story set me thinking…

It was not possible to access Google or any kind of western search engine in China because the Chinese blocked as many western websites as they could and Google was banned outright. But I always put a VPN app on my phone and computer before leaving the UK which meant I could usually bypass the Chinese censorship by accessing Singapore, Tokyo or Los Angeles via satellite. As all my emails were google ones, it was essential to be able to open them – especially for utility bills etc. I say I could 'usually bypass' because it was a daily battle between the Chinese internet censorship teams trying to block the American VPN program, and the Americans counter-attacking to get round the blockades as quickly as they could.

I typed 'The Inn of the Sixth Happiness' into Google and saw that happily there were no problems that day. I knew the film was based on a true story of an English woman who led about a hundred Chinese orphans over a mountain to escape from the Japanese – but not much more than that. I was very surprised to read that the mountain was in Yangchen County, Shanxi Province, just across the Yellow River from Luoyang – in fact, not far from where we were on Song Mountain. The English woman's name was Gladys Aylward and the date of her courageous act was 1938, a year after the Japanese had invaded China.

With Michael's help I then questioned Shifu, his wife and Lijuan about the dates of their village attacks – there were a few – and after a lot of discussion (the event was before both Shifu and his wife were born) Lijuan finally worked out that the date was – 1938!

For me it was really special to be experiencing so much history on such a personal level. Life was infinitely rich here on Song Mountain, so steeped in traditions in which much courage had been shown.

ॐ

I was enjoying meeting the ten foreign students, from five different countries, now at the school. I and Michael got many questions about everything, but there was one question on everybody's lips: where could they have a Chinese massage? Both Michael and I smiled because this was a common question, and of course we had an answer – a good answer!

In order to help blind people in China, the communist government had initiated a scheme of establishing massage shops/parlours/clinics on basically every block in Chinese towns. Instead of being left to a life of inertia, uselessness and poverty, blind people could train as masseurs at government expense, and once qualified, they would be set up in one of these massage clinics to earn a living. (In fact this was also a common practice in old China and Japan.) Rent and equipment were provided by the government. The Chinese are very fond of having a massage and it is a popular lunch time activity. For a westerner having a good massage here was very cheap – a couple of pounds – and, after a hard day's training, kungfu students loved to have their tired aching muscles worked over. It was also an introduction for them to some forms of traditional Chinese medicine.

The Gulun Kungfu school patronised a really lovely blind man, Yuofeng, and his wife, whose little massage shop was spotlessly clean and tidy. He was the main practitioner while she, who wasn't blind, did the business side of things and looked after people when they entered.

Yuofeng also did Moxa treatments – a traditional Chinese medicine therapy which consists of burning dried mugwort (artemisia) either over or directly onto particular acupuncture points on the body – and cupping therapy, which is an ancient form of traditional medicine in which special cups are put on the skin for a few minutes to create suction. It is used to help with pain, inflammation, blood flow, relaxation and well-being, and as a type of deep-tissue massage.

Yuofeng and his wife most definitely profited, deservedly, by being patronised by western kungfu students and by myself and my visiting western friends, and I therefore thought very sadly of them and so many small businesses like shops selling kungfu paraphernalia, popular tea shops, small convenience stores, one-family restaurants, small taxi firms, even street food vendors – as well as, of course, the extended Wu Family – when the devastating events described below started to unfold.

The first intimation that something was wrong was when Michael and three other foreign students arrived at my flat one morning and told me that something strange, possibly threatening, was happening at the kungfu school. Less than an hour before, their kungfu lesson had suddenly been stopped and they had been told to leave immediately and either go and train in the surrounding forests or disappear into town. They were also told to go via the back path through the forest and not via the usual dirt road going down from the school to the main road and Shilipu village.

This was worrying. Over the past few weeks both YaJun, and Yaofeng at the convenience store, had told me that something strange had been happening with kungfu in Dengfeng. As far as I could make out, the government had recently decided that kungfu should be designated as a sport only, and that any religious affiliations should be ended, forcibly if necessary. This was serious for the whole kungfu tradition but catastrophic for Gulun Kungfu which is based on Zen and meditation. Were we entering yet one more period of spiritual persecution by this current government?

After the students left, I called Lijuan and asked her what was happening. She said that government officials were due at the school any moment and everybody was very nervous as they did not know what the officials would do. Other small schools in the area had been forcibly closed and the students sent home. Something like this would be a disaster for the Wu family as the extended family was dependent on the income from the school.

Twice in the past, Shifu had asked me to be present at the school when officials came to visit, because it gave him a certain status to have visiting foreigners there, obviously interested in what he was doing. I wasn't sure if this would be a good idea in this situation but I asked Lijuan if I should come up there anyway. She seemed to think it was a good idea and so I quickly went up to the school, having considered that the innate respect that the Chinese have for old people, and also the possible 'brakes' an interested foreigner might have on the actions of the officials, might have some effect.

Arriving at the school there was an atmosphere of tension and fear in the air. Shifu was sitting at a table in the yard with two senior students serving tea, so I joined them. Most of the young students were sitting quietly in their rooms and the western students had vanished.

Within a few minutes, five officials arrived – four men and a woman. Wenju greeted them and there was some discussion, after which a few senior students were called and the violation began. It was a devastating experience watching the visual images of the Gulun Kungfu tradition being dismantled and destroyed. I felt so deeply sorry and concerned for the Master – it felt like his whole life's work was being wiped out in front of his eyes. Everybody knew there was nothing they could do except follow the imperious instructions being issued. To resist could result in more heavy-handed repercussions because these officials had the power to do what they liked.

The officials started with the meditation room and the altar, and instructed the students to remove all signs of worship such as the Bodhi-

Students meditating

dharma scroll, the incense burners, the treasured artifacts and even the fruit offering made that morning – as well as the meditation cushions. Wenju indicated that everything should be stored in a small room at the back of the building.

The officials then entered the Reception Room where Shifu had another small altar, and a huge picture on the wall depicting the Shaolin Temple's famous old wall painting of kungfu, showing Shifu's great-great-grandfather, Master Wu Gulun, and another monk, in a typical

Gulun Kungfu pose (see the chapter title photograph). I wondered why this painting was regarded as a spiritual connection but I supposed that any connection with the Shaolin Temple itself indicated some kind of religious significance. Watching that huge painting being removed really disturbed me – this was the symbol of Gulun Kungfu and the tradition of generations of the Wu family. Many photos of Shifu's ancestors on the walls were also removed.

Shifu and author in front of a copy of the old Shaolin Temple wall-painting

Once satisfied, the officials then went into all rooms, private and public, in the building to see if there were any further signs of Zen or Buddhist affiliations. Actually there weren't, so they contented themselves with orders to remove a few remaining photos, showing the lineage of Shifu's ancestors, starting with Master Wu Gulun and ending

with Shifu and Wenju, which were hung at the small entrance hall of the building.

The final indignity came when one official spotted some calligraphy on the concrete podium where demonstrations were often given. The calligraphy denoted 'ChanWuYi', one of the traditional kungfu concepts, meaning something like 'awareness' (in this case Zen), movement of the body and medicine. According to these officials 'Wu' and 'Yi' were acceptable but 'Chan' was not and they demanded that this symbol be destroyed. Eventually some left-over concrete was brought, mixed with water, and the symbol was concreted over.

The officials then seemed to feel that the job was done, but they had one last parting shot: students would no longer be allowed to wear the traditional kungfu uniform but now had to wear everyday modern clothes when training. They then departed.

ೞ

We were all in shock and I felt immense sorrow that this tradition that had existed for over fifteen hundred years was being exterminated. This was the latest manifestation of the religious persecution and cultural destruction that has plagued China for millennia – the horrors of the Cultural Revolution were still in living memory, and it seemed that nothing had changed.

At the time, I breathed one sigh of relief that at least the school – the Wu family's life work – had not been closed, but only a week later came the shattering news that the school had indeed been ordered to close and all students were to be sent home. My concern was two-fold: this beautiful tradition was being destroyed in front of my eyes and, secondly, what would the family do for an income? They had no other means of support.

It was eerie to be visiting the now deserted school building. It seemed, however, that one small reprieve had been granted: the foreign students were allowed to stay and continue their training. This was a relief because it meant that at least the family would have some income. And thankfully Wenju and his family would be allowed to continue to live in the building.

From a Chinese friend unrelated to the school, I got a little more information about the overall situation with all the kungfu schools in Dengfeng. It seemed that, as well as getting rid of any spiritual dimensions, the government was also not satisfied with the general education that the students were getting in the small kungfu schools. The government wanted the children to be more rigorously educated (and brain-washed?) so that they could take their place in the now heavily industrialised, financially-focussed, modern China. The smattering of learning provided at the small schools was not sufficient to equip them for this modernised world. My opinion was that the government could not control what was being fed into the children's minds in small, out-of-the-way schools, whereas in the bigger institutions, like at the Shaolin Temple and Tagore University and one or two other big colleges, the government could dictate the curriculum which would certainly indoctrinate the students effectively with communist theories and policies.

Going into Dengfeng also felt strange and different. Until now I was accustomed to seeing young kungfu students practising everywhere. Kungfu was the number one industry in Dengfeng with, at its peak, as many as four hundred schools. Most of them were quite small without a lot of land so students practised on the street pavements or in parks, or basically in any open space. So they were very much in evidence. Even more disconcerting was the defacement of murals of kungfu and its Buddhist associations on public buildings around the city. Teams of men with tins of paint had been ordered to paint over any kungfu artwork on public walls where there was some religious association.

Public murals being defaced

Then many of the supporting industries that I have mentioned before – small shops selling all the paraphernalia used in kungfu tuition, plus cheap clothes shops and restaurants for so many students, and small hotels for visiting parents – were now quickly going out of business. I wondered if the government gave any compensation to these small, family-run businesses. There was no other industry in Dengfeng except building and road construction, which mostly required fairly specialised skills and/or raw physical strength, neither of which the small shop owners had.

Because summer was approaching it was soon time for me to leave, and once back home in the UK I didn't hear of any further developments.

❦

But when I returned in the autumn, I laughed with relief, realising that I had succumbed too easily to fear of problems for the family. Within days of my arrival, I was very surprised to see that the kungfu school was suddenly full of students and there was lots of activity everywhere.

Nobody could give me any comprehensive explanations (I now had a translating app on my phone which did enable me to communicate a little, although in an infuriatingly inaccurate way) but, by putting together bits and pieces of information, I think I more or less understood what was going on.

It seemed that Shifu and Wenju had been very busy communicating with government authorities, petitioning them to give permission to reopen the school. The education issue had been addressed and a qualified teacher had been engaged to educate the students, and the training schedule revised to an approximate timetable of a real school i.e. less time spent training, more time studying. With no Zen influence visible anywhere, it seemed that the authorities were reasonably sure that the students would not be indoctrinated with the spiritual influences of Zen and Buddhism – maybe Shifu and Wenju had to sign on a relevant dotted line somewhere.

As I said, within days of my arrival, the school was suddenly full of students arriving en masse and taking up residence as if there had been no break. I was rather puzzled over this. Surely it would take some time for old and new students to arrive and for the school's routines to start up again? I was at loss for a while but I finally discovered the answer to the mystery. And I laughed out loud! By adroit management and communal good will between kungfu schools, the Gulun Kungfu school had survived by merely appearing to follow the draconian government orders, while in reality not doing so at all.

What had actually happened was that Shifu had negotiated with one of the bigger wushu schools to house all his students in their buildings in the hope that the strict regulations would eventually be relaxed. So about thirty students (only the very young students were sent home) and two coaches had moved to this other school where they continued to train in Gulun Kungfu. This school had already been investigated by the authorities and given the all clear, so it was unlikely that there would

Students practising back in the school grounds

be any further visits. Obviously accommodation fees were paid to this school – so they benefitted from the arrangement – but the tuition fees still went to the Gulun Kungfu school and the Wu family and the coaches.

I loved this! The people peacefully resisting the punitive communist regime which threatened their lives and livelihoods. It was actually quite awe-inspiring that Shifu and other kungfu managers had quietly made their own arrangements to support each other and to continue their kungfu training in the face of government oppression. I was filled with respect at their courage.

It was inspiring that this kind of rebellious spirit was still alive today. I had heard so many stories of how in the past, people quietly rebelled and continued to exercise their independence during the Cultural

Revolution and I was really delighted to see that the spirit of the people still very much existed in these present times.

Please note: At the time of publishing, despite Covid restrictions, all is now well at the Gulun Kungfu Academy, with the arranged compromises and better educational facilities all adhered to. Foreign students will be allowed to attend once Covid restrictions to visit China are lifted.

9
Wutai Shan

The Great White Pagoda, Tayuan Temple, Wutai Shan

From 'The Heart Sutra'
Translation by Thich Nhat Hanh

Listen Sariputra,
this Body itself is Emptiness
and Emptiness itself is this Body.
This Body is not other than Emptiness
and Emptiness is not other than this Body.
The same is true of Feelings,
Perceptions, Mental Formations,
and Consciousness.

Listen Sariputra,
all phenomena bear the mark of Emptiness;
their true nature is the nature of
no Birth no Death,
no Being no Non-being,
no Defilement no Purity,
no Increasing no Decreasing.

That is why in Emptiness,
Body, Feelings, Perceptions,
Mental Formations and Consciousness
are not separate self-entities.[6]

Wutai Shan

When I first arrived in the rural area around Song Mountain in 2008, there were, apart from bicycles and scooters, basically three kinds of motor vehicles being used on the still rudimentary road system. The automobile prevalent was a Volkswagen Passat based on a 1980's design. It seemed that Volkswagen had not updated their Chinese factories to anything more modern and were, even at this time, still manufacturing this one type of out-dated vehicle.

Then there was a home-manufactured vehicle: a small van or people carrier based on a European design also about thirty years old. It was basic to an extreme.

Thirdly there was one of the weirdest contraptions I have ever seen; certainly it did not exist outside of China. Contraption is the pertinent word. It consisted of a metal cart on two wheels designed to carry goods of any description but mostly used by farmers, a seat for two people, a long chassis with a kind of steering apparatus and a kind of 'outboard' engine by which the vehicle would be driven. Words fail at its weirdness; there is nothing I could compare it to. In addition to its odd appearance, it was extremely noisy and belched clouds of thick smoke out of its rear exhaust.

By about 2012, however, things had changed. Volkswagen still had the greater share of the vehicle market and had updated the design to a slightly more recent model, but Japanese and Korean cars were making a rapid intrusion into what savvy businessmen saw as a whole new market. It was still only the rich, however, who could afford these cars and the majority of them were chauffer driven. Three years later, however, the Chinese had jumped into this lucrative market and started to churn out their own vehicles, copied of course from foreign models. This meant that cars were now affordable for many and a car quickly became the latest status symbol.

Simultaneously the Chinese government invested hugely in a widespread new road system, mostly abandoning any maintenance on the existing roads which originated from a time when animal-drawn vehicles were the norm and were not therefore suitable for motor vehicles.

Amidst this very swift and massive investment in modern forms of rapid transportation, two vital ingredients had been overlooked: the driver and the pedestrian. This resulted in an appalling chaos which drove me and other visiting westerners close to apoplexy. I was used to the mad chaos of traffic in India, but it was sane and calm in comparison to traffic in China at this time. It seemed to me that the Chinese attitude to learning to drive a car was the same as learning to ride a bicycle: you got onto it, had a friend lend an initial hand, wobbled for a while, fell off a few times, and eventually got the hang of it. When the vehicle concerned was a bicycle this was not particularly dangerous, but now that the vehicle was motorised and able to travel at speed, the predictable result was a huge rise in traffic accidents.

And a related problem was that the people who were able to afford cars were middle-aged. They didn't as easily adapt to these rapid changes happening at this time as younger people did, so the roads were full of older people at the steering wheels, weaving their chaotic ways all over the place. It was terrifying. Young people have a better chance of learning to drive efficiently and cope with busy traffic than older people because their reflexes are good and they can learn new skills more rapidly. Certainly the only driver I felt remotely safe with – until the last three years I was in China – was Wenju, who started learning how to drive at seventeen, and whose reflexes were lightning fast. Because Wenju drove me around a lot, most of my hair-raising experiences of hazardous Chinese roads over the years came from driving with him and seeing how he reacted to, and swerved us through, the daily traffic. I guarantee that there are a number of people still alive today due to Wenju's very fast reflexes!

Then there were the pedestrians: from small children, to cell-phone-entranced youngsters heedless of oncoming traffic, to old people who simply had no experience of this new traffic phenomenon and so continued to walk all over the roads as they had always done.

Over the past few years, however, I must say that things have changed. The road network and the vehicles have improved, and with a much-needed mandatory basic driver's licensing system in place, there is now some semblance of a highway code in evidence. Younger drivers are now in the majority because their work opportunities often depend on having driving skills. They are more used to traffic and quicker to react in emergencies. As for the pedestrians, I have recently often driven past groups of younger kids being taught how to cross the busy roads, so there does seem to be increasingly more effort to impart some traffic sense into kids' brains.

⊱⊰

This has been rather a long preamble but I wanted to talk about transportation as it was an essential part of my daily life in China. It was also an important aspect of a rather difficult situation I found myself in when I discussed making a trip to the sacred Buddhist mountain called Wutai Shan with Lijuan.

Although not particularly drawn to it, I was curious about this mountain. Its name appeared constantly when Buddhism was discussed and Yujie had mentioned it as she had been there a few times. At that time, however, I hadn't met any other westerner who had been there so I was curious to see it for myself.

Lijuan was thinking about going there and I suggested that maybe we could plan a visit there together. From where we were, Wutai Shan was not easy to reach as it was tucked away in a rather remote, scarcely-populated area in the mountain range called Taihang, which stretches almost from the west of Beijing, south through Shanxi province and ends in the Song Mountain cluster across the Yellow River.

Lijuan was excited. Her little son was now old enough to be left with his father and grandparents for a few days and I sensed she was keen to have a little time for herself. There was one rather big problem though. It was now almost the end of September and from the 1st to the 7th of

October there is a national holiday and the whole of China is on the move, so any travelling becomes an instantaneous nightmare. It should be avoided, but a few days after the end of the holiday some friends were coming from Singapore to visit me, and also it gets cold very quickly in northern mountainous areas. So our window for travelling was limited. Knowing, however, that most people would have arrived home on the last day of the holiday, I suggested to Lijuan that she try to book us train tickets to leave on that day. This she managed to do (you usually have to book ten days in advance to get a ticket on a Chinese train), and so our plans were made.

Lijuan booking train tickets for our journey

When describing my visits to China to friends, I over and over again use the phrase 'expect the unexpected'. It very relevantly expressed much of my life there, and its aptness – and still one more test of my patience – suddenly emerged when Lijuan called me and asked me to come immediately to the school. On my arrival, Shifu invited me to have some tea and meet a friend of his. With Lijuan translating, it transpired that Shifu would also like to go to Wutai Shan and his friend (who looked about sixty years old) had offered to drive us all there. But as his car was twenty years old – one of those old Volkswagen Passats mentioned earlier – the friend had taken the car into the garage to check if it was roadworthy enough to make the fifteen-hour journey there. If given the okay we would start in two days' time – day one of the upcoming national holiday.

I was horrified! Fifteen hours sitting squashed in an ancient car, the sole driver of which was a sixty-year-old man with a few months of driving experience, travelling on an old, unknown, contorted mountain road on the day that all of China was taking to the roads … I could not think of a greater or more hazardous ordeal. Also, on this trip I wanted to be free to savour this ancient place of pilgrimage how, when, and where I wanted. The very last thing I needed was to deal with the clashing ideas of strangers – let alone be forced to endure their driving. I knew that we would naturally follow Shifu's plans and although he was creative with his ideas and often a lot of fun, still I wanted to do what I wanted to do, and I could sense that Lijuan was also not much in favour of this plan. (I later found out why.)

But … one didn't argue with Shifu. Here the Chinese patriarchal force came into its own. What he said, everyone did! I loved the man but I was fully aware that he could be quite dictatorial – which was confirmed when Lijuan told me she had cancelled the extremely hard-to-get train tickets. To say I was in a dilemma was putting it mildly. According to Chinese protocol there was no way I could refuse Shifu but as far as I could see, this proposal looked like a disaster in the making. While there, Shifu's friend got a phone call and beamingly confirmed that the garage had given their okay for us to make the long drive safely. We were soon to be on our way, it seemed.

Or maybe not. The next day Lijuan came to see me and told me that Shifu had now decided that he didn't have the time to go, so he had cancelled his part in the enterprise. The friend had then said he didn't want to go if Shifu wasn't going – for me it was clearly apparent that he wanted the kudos or prestige of spending time with Shifu and he was not interested in putting out so much effort just for two women. I was very annoyed because now Lijuan had cancelled our train tickets so we were exactly nowhere. She told me she had tried to rebook the tickets on the trains that would fit my time frame but they were all totally full. I thought for a while. Lijuan had done all her ticket booking online and I knew that anyway I would have to go to the local ticket office in Dengfeng to get the actual tickets, because identification was needed and as I didn't have a Chinese ID card, the official in the ticket office had to check my passport and then manually enter an identity approval. So I suggested that we go down to the ticket office and talk to the usually very helpful person there and see if he or she could help.

This we immediately did. The young woman in the office was predictably helpful and vigorously rattled her computer keys to see if she could find a ticketing solution. Suddenly she gave a little shriek and quickly asked Lijuan something. It turned out that she had found one single seat in one carriage and another single seat in a carriage some distance away. Would we be satisfied sitting so far apart? Lijuan, bless her, didn't want to subject me to being alone, but I told her I nearly always travelled alone on trains in China so I didn't mind in the least. Agreement confirmed, the young woman's fingers flew at high speed over her keyboard (at any one time a few million people would be trying to book a ticket on this train at this time, so she had to be fast) and soon she gave a sigh of relief – she had secured both seats for us on the train to a city called Shijiazhuang on the final day of the national holiday (and a return four days later) which fitted comfortably with our schedule. It remained to get two seats on the connecting train from Shijiazhuang to a city called Taiyuan up in the mountains, but as this wasn't a busy train line, that part was easy. I submitted my passport and, much relieved, we left the ticket office, tickets in hand. Job done.

Or was it? The next morning my poor Lijuan came to my flat to pick me up and take me to the school. She had a mutinous look on her face and refused to tell me why. Again Shifu was sitting drinking tea with the friend and, with a beaming smile, Shifu said something in Chinese which Lijuan had to translate. It seemed the friend had changed his mind yet again and had decided he would take us after all, even without Shifu. Shifu looked delighted that he had arranged this successfully.

My heart sank into my shoes and I was actually speechless for a few seconds. I even queried the news, asking Lijuan to repeat what she had said. Knowing neither of the men could understand what I said, I asked Lijuan if this was what she wanted. She – immersed in her Chinese conditioning which requires the child to always follow the parents – told me she didn't want to go with the man but that it was impossible to refuse because Shifu had arranged it. Hmmnnn… From my point of view, it was not impossible to refuse, and I asked her to politely say that we had rebooked new tickets at a time convenient for us and we didn't want to change arrangements yet again. I felt that this stupid man was quite likely to change his mind again and anyway, although I could have borne the hazardous journey if Shifu were there, I was not prepared to do it with a stranger. I had had too many experiences of hazardous driving. Poor Lijuan, she was again caught in the centre of the dilemma. She hesitated, so I took her hand, looked Shifu in the eye and politely, with a nice smile on my face, said in Chinese: 'Duibuqi, bu!' which means: 'I am sorry, no!'

Shifu momentarily looked a bit shocked! He was not used to somebody saying 'no' to him! He questioned Lijuan again and she replied, presumably repeating our position that we had already booked our train tickets again and didn't want to cancel them one more time. She fortunately had the tickets in her bag so I told her to show them to the two men to back up our case.

I could see I was going against all the Chinese conditioning here but by now Shifu had acquired considerable experience of foreigners doing things differently and he was also dealing with someone twenty years older than himself (luckily for me, age counts in China) – so after a few minutes he nodded, produced a smile and said: 'Hen hao' which in the local Henan dialect means 'very good', and which he knew I would understand. And I knew too that there would be no hard feelings because he was a gracious, generous, far-seeing man and could accept the inevitable.

No further rearrangements arose to hinder our plans so within a few days Lijuan and I were on our way.

જ•◌

I don't know much about Wutaishan because very little seems to have been written about it in English (compared, for example, to Song Mountain and Dunhuang). And information from Chinese friends had been rather sketchy. Most of the online information about the place has been posted by tourist agencies in China which naturally focus on activities for tourists, and give little more than a rudimentary nod to its sacred Buddhist history. What little information I have been able to gather is as follows.

Mount Wutai, or Wutai Shan, is a cluster of five flat-topped mountain peaks or terraces in the north eastern province of Shanxi. ('Wu' means five, 'tai' means terrace and 'shan' means mountain.)

Because of its remote situation, it is difficult to reach, which probably explains why not many foreign tourists, even if they are religious enthusiasts, go there. While I was there, I saw only two other western people – in contrast to the Song Mountain and Dunhuang areas of spiritual and historical significance, where there are always at least a few. It is even more difficult to reach from the south, the direction we would be travelling from, than from Beijing in the north, which is why I had never been there and wouldn't have gone without Lijuan's help.

Wutai Shan is famous as one of the great holy places of Buddhism. Great numbers of temples, including some of the oldest wooden buildings surviving in China, are scattered over the mountain. The largest temples – such as Xiantong, Tayuan, Shuxiang and Pusading – are grouped around the town of Taihuai Zhen, which is where we stayed. Needless to say, we saw only a handful of the temples in the short time we were there.

The questions that spring to mind is how did people reach this remote spot in the first place – and why did they go there? Part of the answer is that the Taoists, who are well-known for seeking out remote mountain peaks on which to build their temples and monasteries, had apparently long ago penetrated this almost impenetrable mountain range and had decided that the valley, surrounded by its five flat-topped peaks, was an auspicious place to live and worship. Then during the later Wei Dynasty period (386–535), it somehow became identified by the Chinese as the dwelling place of Manjushri (Chinese: Wenshu) who was considered to be the oldest and most significant bodhisattva in Mahāyāna Buddhism. By this time Buddhism was popular throughout China.

During the next five or six hundred years, pilgrims and scholars flocked to the area and a total of about four hundred temples were constructed.

In the ninth century some Zen Buddhism monasteries were built and, because they had the patronage of the provincial governors of the neighbouring areas of Hebei, Wutai Shan was protected from the worst ravages of the great religious persecution that occurred from 841 to 845.

Then, in the thirteenth century, when part of China was under Mongol rule, Tibetan Buddhism was introduced and appropriate temples were built around the older temples in the valley. The importance of Tibetan Buddhism remains to this day. As I mentioned before, the symbol of Wutai Shan, the great White Tower, is actually a Tibetan stupa similar to architecture I saw when visiting Nepal and Kathmandu. I noticed many Tibetan pilgrims during my short time in Wutai Shan.

With its hundreds of lavishly endowed temples and monasteries, dedicated to Taoism and different sects of Buddhism, it is no wonder that Wutai Shan was a place of enormous significance. The significance has now declined, no doubt accelerated by the Cultural Revolution and recent attempts at religious persecution, and only about fifty-three temples now remain, many of them in remote areas and in poor condition except for the ones already mentioned, centred around Taihuai Zhen.

The architectural feats of the religious buildings of Wutai Shan are of considerable historical importance; for example, the main hall of Foguang Temple, dating from 857, is one of the oldest surviving wooden buildings in China; and Shuxiang Temple, said to be Manjushri's 'house', has an astonishing complex of five hundred three-dimensional statues attached to the walls and ceiling, which represent Buddhist stories. Because these historically important buildings record the way Buddhist architecture developed and influenced other buildings throughout China and Asia, Mount Wutai was designated a UNESCO World Heritage Site in 2009.

❦❧

Now that our plans were finally settled, Lijuan set about organising our departure, and did a brilliant job. With so many private cars now on the roads, a system of individual 'taxi' rides had been set up, accessed on the Chinese WeChat app., so, whereas in former years a taxi ride to Zhengzhou – from where we would catch the train to Shijiazhuang – might cost between 200 or 500 yuan (£24 to £55 – depending on the honesty of the taxi driver), a young driver could now collect four or five passengers in Dengfeng and take everybody to the big city, about an hour's drive away, for an average of about 30 yuan (£3.50) per person, and would do the same thing on his return journey, thus making a nice little untaxed income for himself. Petrol is very cheap in China because it is subsidised by the government.

Our competent young driver that Lijuan had engaged took us directly to the huge railway station where we easily boarded our train: one of the new, very comfortable, super-efficient and very luxurious high-speed ones. Lijuan showed her organisational skills to be pure gold when she found a kind man sitting near her who was willing to exchange his seat for mine so I could sit next to her for the journey to Shijiazhuang. The transfer to the local train went without a hitch and I settled down contentedly … only to jerk upright in shock as we exited a very long tunnel into a thick, dark cloud of pollution! I was appalled. Although I knew this area to be one of the most polluted in China due to the huge coal mines and associated power stations generating electricity, I wasn't prepared for the reality of the dense black smog we were travelling through. I used to think that Zhengzhou was bad but this was something else. After what seemed like ages, we entered another long tunnel, and finally, to my relief, emerged into bright, clear sunlight.

Once out of the tunnel Lijuan became very occupied with her phone and a lot of intense conversations ensued. The outcome I soon discovered was that plans had changed due to the kind intervention of the manager of the small hotel in Wutai Shan that Lijuan had booked us into. After arriving in Taiyuan, we were now to take a taxi to a certain point from where we would be picked up by a local driver who had set up the same WeChat-run taxi system of picking up passengers in his own private car. This was rather a relief because otherwise we would have had to take a bus which left from another station on the other side of this very large crowded city. We ended up standing for about twenty minutes on the fly-over of a big highway but, sure enough, a car soon drew up and a cheerful man gently pushed us into his car with two other people and we were off. Sadly it was now getting dark and I couldn't see the scenery but anyway we quickly drove into a very long tunnel – called the Fenghuangling Tunnel – which has to be the longest I have ever been through. Allegedly one of the longest tunnels in China, it still didn't quite compare with the longest Swiss or European tunnels.

Having dropped off his other passengers, the driver kindly took us straight to our small, very basic hotel run by two brothers. They managed to provide some soup and steamed bread for us, after which both Lijuan and I retired to our respective rooms and fell asleep.

In the morning I found there was fortunately mildly warm water in the small shower room, and met Lijuan as I left my room and went to the little dining room for breakfast. Ooops! It turned out that we were much too early (due to our Song Mountain habits of rising around 5.30 am) and neither of the two brothers had woken up yet. I love the informality of the Chinese! Lijuan banged on the guys' bedroom door and obviously told them in no uncertain terms that we were ready for breakfast. There were a few yells in reply.

I am sure we weren't very popular but food arrived fairly soon at the table, served by one of the brothers, still in his pyjamas. There must have been someone in the kitchen because we got the standard unappetising millet gruel and the tasteless traditional steamed bread. The only saving grace for me was a hard-boiled egg which was grudgingly increased to two at my request. This rather minimal fare once eaten, we quickly set off because we wanted an early start to see as much as possible in the short time we had.

We had been told that at the end of the road we could take a bus into town and I enjoyed the walk in the cold but crystal-clear mountain air. The sun was barely rising over the mountains to the east, so we were treated to some diffused sunrise colours on the opposite mountain peaks.

When we arrived at the bus stop, we found we were going to share the vehicle with about fifteen nuns with shaved heads and brown robes. They greeted us with smiles and the Buddhist *amituofu* (Amitabha Buddha) greeting and chatted all the way with Lijuan. The whole scene was quite fascinating and as we entered the small town of Taihuai where all the main temples were clustered, we were rewarded with the impressive sight of the main Wutai Shan symbol: the Great White Pagoda, of distinct Tibetan design.

The Pagoda highlighted by the rays of the rising sun

A Chinese tourist website writes that this temple houses a collection of Shakyamuni's *sharira* sent to China by the benevolent Indian Buddhist Emperor, Ashoka. Shakyamuni, another name for Buddha, is the founder of Buddhism and *sharira* are crystalline remains of the body of an enlightened person after he is cremated – sacred relics worthy of veneration.

The Great White Pagoda also contains some hairs of Manjushri so it is an even more important monument – although as Manjushri was a mythical Buddhist deity and not a person as Buddha was, it is hard to believe that the hairs belong to him! (I found that the Chinese seemed to be very confused about Manjushri and when I said that he was a mythical god and not a real person, they got round that by saying: 'Ah, but he often manifested himself as a real person or animal' – specifically as an old man and sometimes even a fox.) However, it seems to be that the significant point for pilgrims to this mountain is that it is the very precious earthly home of Manjushri and I was to find that most temples have some association with him.

But before actually reaching the Pagoda, part of the Taiyuan Temple, we had to pass by what I think was the Foguang Temple mentioned above. Maybe because so few foreigners visit this place, none of the signs anywhere were written in English so I had only a nominal idea about what I was seeing and Lijuan was able to explain very little. What I was a bit surprised to see, however, was that one of the temples had thousands of little buddhas, in wood, not stone as seen in the Longmen Caves, and Lijuan confirmed that I was looking at some more 'Ten Thousand Buddhas', loved by Osho, and seemingly very popular with Buddhists everywhere in China.

Walking further to get close to the Pagoda I noticed that there were many Tibetan-looking people – their facial features did not resemble the typical Han Chinese. They were also very friendly and, as usual, Lijuan was surrounded by people asking about me, but, from what I could understand, communication was minimal because they were either using dialects or not speaking the same language at all.

Here, in all innocence, I became a 'fleeced' tourist when a very sweet old monk came and sat with me and gave me a lovely wooden mala. I asked Lijuan if I should give him some money and she nodded and I gave him only twenty yuan instead of probably a more acceptable fifty yuan, because I didn't as yet realise that the locals earned their living by

getting as much money out of visitors as possible. Even if Lijuan asked for some simple directions, the person demanded payment and, I found, nothing less than fifty yuan (about five English pounds) was considered to be acceptable. The old monk was very sweet and I didn't mind giving him some money as he didn't demand anything, but this was the beginning of the generally disappointing impression I had of the place: to the monks (were they actual monks or just in costumes?) spirituality was a money-making business and Lijuan, with me as the only foreigner in tow, was constantly being targeted to give money. She took it all in her stride, however, because she was a calm, centred young woman and although it was sometimes annoying for her, she often had quite a good time connecting with strangers curious about me and the other foreign students at the kungfu school. It was obvious that she liked chatting to the charming young monk at the Xiantong temple, and the lovely three Tibetans we later met.

From the Great Pagoda we walked further to the very imposing Xiantong Temple – the oldest surviving temple and the biggest in Wutai Shan – the origins of which were first built in around 68 CE. As the first Buddhists came to China, to Luoyang, in around 67 CE, they must have moved quickly to Wutai Shan. I remember Yujie telling me this but she was flummoxed when I asked her how did these early Buddhists know about this place because at the time it was only a small Taoist centre? She finally said they had memories of it from past lives and so were guided there. Well, that was a rather unusual explanation but perhaps she was right because I have since found an account in Wikipedia:

Apparently the association of Mañjuśrī with Wutai (Wu-t'ai) Shan in north China was known in classical times in India itself, identified by Chinese scholars with the mountain in the 'north-east' (when seen from India or Central Asia) referred to as the abode of Mañjuśrī in the 'Avataṃsaka Sūtra' which was written in approximately 300 BCE. In this great work there is a passage which describes the abodes of many bodhisattvas, Mañjuśrī being one of them. It said that he lived on a 'clear cold mountain' in the northeast of China.

Or perhaps somebody had a vision of the mountain?! There was very little travel between India and China at that time, and probably even less factual knowledge about the place, but, because those early Buddhist monks had some idea about a mystical abode attributed to Manjushri, it would have been fairly easy for them when they arrived in Luoyang to have found out about the location of Wutai Shan from the local Taoists. The Luoyang area was a centre of Taoist spiritual activity – nearby was the awesome Taoist mountain, Huashan, and the town of Sanmenxia where Lao Tzu supposedly wrote his Tao Te Ching. Lao Tzu reportedly worked in the local government offices in Luoyang for a time.

The Xiantong Temple was a splendid one and obviously very rich because there were many statues and decorations covered, according to Lijuan, in real gold. Certainly they shone in the bright sunlight to the point of blinding one's eyes.

Xiantong Temple housing ten thousand gold buddhas

Lijuan then led me into a small building, covered totally in gold, and, to my surprise, I saw thousands of small golden Buddhas covering the walls. It looked just like the cave in the Longmen Caves, although there the buddhas were in stone; here they were in gold.

There was a young, initially disinterested, monk reading something but he got upset when I pulled out my camera. Apparently photos were not allowed in this holy place. I was disappointed because one of my spiritual quests in China was to trace the incidences and hopefully origins of, and reasons for, the 'ten thousand buddhas' mentioned so often by Osho. I asked Lijuan to translate one or two questions I wanted to ask the monk and I could see he was quite surprised at a westerner knowing enough about Buddhism to ask such relevant questions. He put down his book, stood up and began talking animatedly to Lijuan, obviously asking who I was and how I knew enough to ask about these things. Lijuan, bless her, gave him a brief history about me because I heard the words 'India', 'Osho', and my name, Veena. At this the young monk got quite excited and gestured to the camera still in my hand. Lijuan told me that she had explained my situation to him and when he heard that I had – in Lijuan's words – a Buddhist name, he gave permission for me to photograph the ten thousand small golden buddhas in this small room. A special favour!

Apparently he was amazed at a foreigner having such an unusual story. And so I am the proud owner of a unique photo which possibly no other westerner has got. My special scoop!

As I said before, I was surprised by how many temples here had halls dedicated to thousands and thousands of buddhas made from stone, wood and gold. Having seen only the one small cave in the Longmen Grottoes in Luoyang, I hadn't realised how important this concept was to Buddhism. And to Zen too. Something the young monk had said stayed with me. When I asked him what was the reason for so many buddhas, he said that the number was to symbolise that the buddha was not something outside, not **the** Buddha, but that there was a buddha inside everybody so each little statue was a symbol of each one of us. The hope was that the powers of so many buddhas close together would help each one of us realise our own buddha nature and that of everybody else's – with the result that harmony and peace would reign between all people on this earth.

He was so interested, interesting and charming that I forgave some of the other aggressive money-oriented monks, and my heart was even further touched when, exiting the entrance to the Temple complex, I saw three beautiful-looking people in front of me. They were obviously not Chinese and Lijuan confirmed they were Tibetans. One was a little boy who looked about ten years old and he got very excited at seeing me – I was probably the first westerner he had ever seen. He came running up to me and responded when I bowed to him with a 'namaste' gesture (hands together as in prayer). Lijuan replied happily to the questions asked by one of the other monks, obviously well-educated and speaking a form of Chinese she could understand. Really, this was one of the highlights of my time there – these three were so gentle and sweet, very different to the aggressive Chinese monks by whom we were now so often being 'assaulted'. And, when on two more occasions we met this trio, the little monk came running up to me and took my hand and laughingly walked hand-in-hand with me for as long as he could. I was so very touched by his innocence and joy.

Charming Tibetan monks

❧❧

Soon it was lunch time and, having had only a very meagre breakfast, we ate a more filling meal of noodles served listlessly in a small restaurant, before returning to the hotel to rest. I had broken my ankle five weeks before leaving for China, and my leg muscles were still quite weak from weeks of forced inactivity.

After arriving at the hotel and sitting in my room drinking some green tea I had brought with me, I finally got to hear the full explanation of Lijuan's agenda for coming here. It seems she had a WeChat friend (like a Facebook friend) whom she had never met but with whom she had been communicating for about two years. The friend had told her about a 'master' she had met in Wutai Shan and of whom she was now a disciple. Apparently she had told Lijuan that this man had helped her with some personal problems and it transpired that Lijuan wanted to meet him. I was a little surprised but was happy to support her in her quest to find this master and talk to him.

She had apparently been in touch with him by phone and had been invited to visit him. It further transpired that our little hotel had been chosen, on the advice of the WeChat friend, because the master lived only a block away. So I lay down for a nap while Lijuan went off on her quest.

About an hour later Lijuan called me and said that the master wanted to meet me and would I come and visit him. Of course I would, so, following her directions, I finally arrived at his rather 'poor' little dwelling place which was, in contrast, astonishingly filled with at least twenty huge vases of pink/red/white lilies which had apparently been sent by air from southern China by one of his devotees!

There were two other ladies there and we all had a rather unsuccessful conversation because Lijuan was not able to translate so much. Then the master – he looked to me to be in his late thirties and was quite good looking which probably explained his popularity – stood up and announced that we were going for a ride. I was happy to hear this because whenever I was in a heavily touristic area, I really liked to go off the beaten track and do something different. He had a rather nice 'people-carrier' van into which we all climbed and we set off on a small road in the opposite direction of the town. It was quite beautiful driving up into some low mountains and through some rural villages until we eventually arrived at a small hamlet. We were then led to a good-sized building still under construction. This, I learnt, was a kind of small monastery the master was building where he could hold meditation retreats with his disciples. Although still in the construction phase, it looked well-designed and attractive.

This young man was charismatic and intelligent and, I felt, also ambitious, and I wondered whether he was a genuine article or jumping on the bandwagon of making money by playing the priest and cashing in on some gullible people – all women by the look of things. Or is that my cynical mind talking? And, on the other hand, if people are helped and comforted, who am I to judge? To be honest, I would have liked to have been able to do a meditation retreat in his little mountain monastery.

It was full moon that night so Lijuan and I had a slow wander up a small road near our little hotel and savoured the lovely rays of the silver moon. A full moon in the mountains is always a special event. Lijuan seemed happier too; I hoped the master had helped her to sort some things out for herself.

The next morning, we again rose early but this time an old lady, probably the cook, was ready to give us the same paltry breakfast. We took the bus to a further stop because we wanted to visit the Shuxiang Temple: Manjushri's earthly 'home'.

This was quite an impressive place, being rather large and built on a hill surrounded by many huge trees. Lijuan translated the information board for me and we learned that this temple contained the tallest statue of Manjushri in China and was also famous for the rather unique phenomenon of 'The Five Hundred Arhats Crossing the River' (disciples who gathered together to compile the Buddha's teachings into sutras and also spread his message). These are apparently 'the finest painted sculptures in Wutai Shan'. It is very hard to describe them: they are about two or three feet high, made apparently of brightly-coloured concrete, but are attached to the wall and the ceiling by their feet or back of their legs. It is quite disconcerting to be surrounded by all these very lifelike sculptures. It is also difficult to see them properly because the press of the crowd behind you shunts you so rapidly past them that you can't stop, even for a minute or two, to examine and appreciate them more closely.

Shuxiang Temple, earthly home of Bodhisattva Manjushri

Once outside I found a rare bench and sat down for a little rest while Lijuan explored further. Actually, I wanted to have a few minutes to close my eyes and see if I could feel any kind of 'spiritual energy' here. Song Mountain is such an energy centre that you start to feel suffused with a soft energy as you approach the mountain, even before you see it. It is this energy which has attracted seekers and pilgrims for over two thousand years and which I recognise each time I come here. One feels like one is surrounded by a soft cloud of light the whole time – it is so tangible it almost feels like you can reach out and touch it with your finger-tips.

But in Wutai Shan, China's most sacred Buddhist site, I could feel nothing, not even in this Temple which I rather liked. There was a very different energy here – it seemed as if even the local residents felt nothing for the heritage of Buddhism. They gave the impression that it was just a place to earn their living and that they cared neither for the place nor the pilgrims visiting. Apart from the temples, the ordinary buildings were the same depressing, grey, concrete boxes found in Shilipu village and all over China, the local people were rude and uninterested, and everywhere you could see a lack of care, a lack of aesthetics and a huge amount of litter.

I confess I was disappointed. Just as the great medieval cathedrals in Europe were an inspiring testimony to Christianity, so the temples of Wutai Shan reflected a truly awesome and inspirational devotion to Buddhism. But now it felt to me that this great spiritual endeavour of building hundreds of temples in honour of Buddha, had been reduced to a kind of Disney World, with the intent only to make as much money out of tourism and commercialism as possible. As a centre of devout pilgrimage, it lacked that special uplifting ambience which I was soon to discover again when I visited Dunhuang, where this almost magical phenomenon made itself felt even as the taxi pulled away from the airport.

I didn't share my feelings with Lijuan – I hoped she was experiencing something different because I know how much she had wanted to come here. And it is my own opinion anyway which is of course not necessarily that of anybody else.

To visit the next temple, or more correctly, group of temples, called Pusading, we had to take a taxi to a place on the opposite side of the valley. Here we saw that there was a terrifyingly steep road up to the top of the mountain but, fortunately, there was also a cable car. Lijuan decided to walk – she is a very fit young woman – while I had a really nice shortish ride in the cable car up to the top.

But for me the view from the top was disappointing. Again I could not help but compare it with the awe-inspiring, majestic, stunning Song Mountain. The views here were tame in comparison, and in the town in the valley below you could see the ugly sprawl of grey concrete buildings I mentioned earlier. The word 'picturesque' could never spring to mind.

The temples of Pusading themselves were very well taken care of and beautiful and in one I was happy to listen to some monks chanting. This was the first hint of religiousness I had experienced here!

But once again I reflected on the strange construction of Chinese temples. You are not allowed to go inside nor sit down and meditate, as in a church. Rather you stand at the entrance, marvel at the ornately decorated altar, do your regulation bows ... and leave. There is no possibility of quietly absorbing the spirit of the place. People look, but their hearts are not engaged.

In fact, the only time my feelings were really engaged (apart from meeting the little Tibetan boy) was when we returned to our small hotel and found it packed with people in brown robes (a kind of uniform donned for a sacred happening) busily moving the dining room furniture out of the way. On enquiry, Lijuan found out that this group of people regularly came from another town, first to visit the temples and then in the evening to perform a rather touching ritual together: the chanting of 'The Heart Sutra' and other Buddhist sutras. It was very sweet and we both sat in silence and enjoyed the meditation. But I rather sadly reflected on how these very sincere pilgrims had to do their chanting in a hotel dining room rather than in a temple, or at least somewhere that might enhance the meditative space they were trying to create.

We left early the next morning with the same taxi driver we had come with. I saw more of this mountain area in the early morning light but remained mostly untouched by it. The journey back home to Song Mountain was comfortable and uneventful, but as we approached the mountain, the rather flat feelings I had about where we had just been, vanished like fog in bright sunlight. I felt my heart expand and swell with joy as we re-entered the 'energy field' of this, for me, very sacred place.

10
The Ten Thousand Buddhas

The Library Cave and precious documents
in the Mogao Caves in Dunhuang

Remember that you are only a watcher.
You are neither the body nor the mind,
but only a mirror reflecting,
without any judgment,
a pure reflection of the moon in the lake.
This is your ultimate reality.
This is your very being.
It is beyond words, but not beyond experience.
It is your very sky, without any limitations.
This fortunate evening,
ten thousand buddhas have disappeared
into an oceanic awareness –
just pure consciousness.

Osho

The Ten Thousand Buddhas

On my return to Shilipu village I slipped happily back into the mellow relaxed days I loved so much. With each minute of each day there was much to savour as my time here was soon to end. My flat's balcony and the supremely comfortable chair was my focal point. I loved to sit there at any time of the day, although a chill had started to descend on my early morning and evening meditations. But during the day I could soak up the sun and the mountain's primordial presence.

The trip to Wutai Shan had, however, resurrected a memory and a long-term query. While there, I had encountered numerous instances of the phrase that had haunted me since my first visit here – 'the ten thousand buddhas' – and I reminded myself that I had one more quest to fulfil: to find out more about the origins of the phrase and try to fathom what Osho's meaning – or perhaps his intention – was when he uttered these words.

'The ten thousand buddhas' was a phrase he used frequently in his discourses in his later years, but I never thought much about it except for a passing reflection that we were only about one thousand people sitting in Buddha Hall. So for me his phrase was nothing more than another endearing example of his eternal optimism, his over-flowing generosity and his sense of abundance in all and everything.

I was stunned, therefore, when, during my first visit to China in 2008, I noticed a sign in the famous Longmen Caves near Luoyang which said: 'The Cave of the Ten Thousand Buddhas'! Osho's words! How could this be? The cave was a small one – perhaps eight people could fit into it – and around its walls were painted or carved thousands of small buddhas, some only about two inches high. No other cave in this extraordinary monument to Buddhism, consisting of many caves and statues cut into a hillside, was 'decorated' in this way.

As the months passed, I researched Osho's discourses but could find no explanation of the phrase, other than at one point he mentioned a temple, or temples, filled with thousands of Buddhas where many people could worship. But this was confusing, because his description didn't fit with the one small cave I had discovered.

Further research revealed that the first use of the phrase seems to have originated in about the fourth century when a Buddhist monk named Yuezun (Chinese name), on his way from India to China, had a vision of a place of worship filled with thousands of images of Buddha. He had stopped in the famous desert town of Dunhuang, in Gansu province, on the edge of the Gobi Desert. At the time, Dunhuang was an important trade and commercial hub on the Old Silk Road, probably because of its oasis – a crescent-shaped lake – which to this day has never dried up.

Yuezun was inspired by his vision to start carving out caves in a long hillside beside a river just outside of Dunhuang as a fitting place to worship. (Perhaps on his journey he had also visited the Buddhist caves carved into the hillside behind the great Buddha in Bamiyan, Afghanistan?) Other travelling monks joined him and a large Buddhist settlement developed. Over the next thousand years, more and more caves were formed, filled with exquisite paintings and sculptures, to inspire meditation and enlightenment. Money poured in from rich donors anxious to be connected to this huge spiritual happening and no doubt hoping for redemption of their souls. Some of the caves were large enough for thirty to forty people to worship in. Were these the temples Osho was referring to?

Osho had once mentioned that he had walked with Bodhidharma in a past life and talked about a forest and a cave where Bodhidharma was meditating. As I said in my previous book, the word 'shaolin' means small forest and we know the cave was in the Shaolin Temple area on Song Mountain, not far from Luoyang and the Longmen Caves. If Osho had wandered there at that time, it is conceivable (the dates fit) that Osho would have known about the Longmen Caves and even visited them, thus hearing the phrase 'the ten thousand buddhas'. Dunhuang is far from Luoyang, but with visiting monks continually arriving in the Luoyang area from India via the famous Silk Road, it is also conceivable that he could have heard tales of the caves in Dunhuang from them, and known that they were much bigger and could justifiably be called temples.

One small point… In the original phrase only *one* thousand buddhas were mentioned but by the time it reached Luoyang, the Yungang Grottoes and Wutai Shan (both in Shanxi Province), the number had grown to *ten* thousand buddhas. Osho, with his wonderful largesse obviously preferred the higher number – why, after all, have one thousand buddhas when you can have ten thousand?

☙◦❧

In a few days the friends who were working in Singapore, were coming to visit me but there was time before I departed from the mountain and China for the last time, to take a short trip to Dunhuang. The logistics of the journey were, however, quite daunting and I was nervous about travelling on my own but could not find anyone to go with me. I had suggested it to Michael but he said he could not afford the travel costs.

With all these details floating around in my head I decided to go for a walk and stop off at Yaofeng's village store to buy some supplies. He usually had very good free-range eggs from a local farmer and the best peanuts I have ever eaten. The area around Kaifeng, which is not very far away, on the other side of Zhengzhou, was the most important peanut growing area in China. With the Yellow River depositing its rich layers of silt year after year, the soil was apparently ideal for producing top-quality peanuts. They were definitely good.

Nibbling a few of these peanuts I made my way past the store down to the bus stop where my local vendor friends had their small sesame bun shop. Although we couldn't converse much, they were interested to hear that I had just returned from Wutai Shan and we sat and 'chatted' companionably (although me uncomfortably) on the small stools they provided for their customers. Then, when a bus arrived from Dengfeng, out stepped Michael. As he was always hungry, he too bought a hot bun, enjoyed a little chat with the vendors and then together we walked back up the hill.

He had news. He told me that he had just been to see his friends in the local tea shop and over a cup of green tea, he told them of his thoughts about going to Dunhuang (so I had sown a seed!) but that the cost was too much. The young man there, son of the owner and now the manager of that branch of their business, immediately opened up his mobile phone and started looking for trains and their fares. I know that there is a vast amount of information online in Chinese that hasn't been translated into English and is therefore not available to foreign tourists, so I wasn't surprised when Michael said that his friend immediately came up with a train journey and fare that was radically cheaper than anything he had managed to find. His friend also said he would buy the ticket for him and that Michael could repay him in cash – because a Chinese credit card was needed to book on this website. Michael was excited but said that he had to consult with me first. There was one train every day which left Zhengzhou at 9.30am and arrived in Dunhuang at 8.30 the next morning. Twenty-three hours!

I was delighted at finding a travelling companion. Despite being exactly half my age, Michael and I had already been good friends for three or four years and he was an intelligent and charming man who loved the unusual. That he could also speak Chinese was a major bonus. Old granny here could not, however, manage twenty-three hours on the train and wanted to fly. Whereas Michael could speak Chinese, my expertise in the partnership was online research, so I suggested he came to my flat where I could check online to see if I could find a flight which would fit in with this new train journey his friend had discovered for him. We decided on a date two weeks ahead. I already knew I would need to fly from Xi'an (home of the famous Terracotta Army) but needed to find appropriate dates and times and an appropriate connecting train from Luoyang.

I found what looked like possible air and rail connections but I also could not book online without a Chinese credit card. However, being travel savvy, this wasn't a problem and I immediately called Trip.com, formerly Ctrip.com, which I had used since my first trip to China in 2008. I was a member and a frequent user, so when I spoke to the young agent (all their frontline staff have to speak good English) she immediately found my records and was ready to help. I told her my travel needs and suggested return plane and train times but asked her to check everything. This she did in about two minutes, agreed that the times and connections were good and confirmed that seats were available on all four sections of the journey.

But we still had to co-ordinate with Michael's friend – it was no good me booking flights if he couldn't get a ticket on the relevant train. So I quickly asked the young woman if she could hold those bookings for me for an hour to allow Michael to confirm with his friend. I knew from past experience that the agent could do this and she agreed, so I took the provisional booking number and rang off. Michael immediately phoned the tea shop friend to see if there was a seat and sleeper bed available on the date we wanted. Within a minute or two the answer came back, yes. Michael asked him to book the tickets for him, and once that was done I called Trip.com back and confirmed the booking and paid with my credit card. One of the reasons this company grew so big and was so efficient was that from the very beginning they saw a gap in the market where foreigners needed to pay with foreign credit cards – so they arranged their payment system accordingly (via Hong Kong apparently) and cleverly captured the market for foreign tourism.

The whole process took less than ten minutes! There can be no other country in the world as efficient at making travel arrangement of all kinds as China.

Three more details still had to be taken care of. The first was to ask my landlord, who ran a small private taxi service doing long-distance journeys to Zhengzhou or Luoyang, if he could take me to the Luoyang train station – and pick me up again. He was happy to, but we would have to leave at 5.00am which was not a problem for either of us as we were both early risers. The second was to take our phones with our booking arrangement confirmed, down to the local ticket office and get the actual tickets for the trains. I could simply use my phone for the plane tickets. That presented no problems. The third was to find a place to stay in Dunhuang. I looked on Booking.com to see if I could find a cheap hotel and found what looked to be a nice youth hostel, very cheap because it was off-season. I showed Michael and he agreed the place looked good so I immediately booked two rooms through Booking.com where again I could use my credit card. We were ready! I can't say how much I was looking forward to this exotic trip.

ൠൠ

Two days later my very dear friends arrived and I happily became a tour guide and showed them all the places I loved so much. With each visit to each place there was an added poignancy for me because I knew I would probably not see these places ever again.

After my friends left I had only two days to get myself organised and packed before the great day arrived. Michael left the day before me and had actually arrived in Dunhuang while I was waiting to catch my flight in Xi'an. He sent me a text: 'Veena, I LOVE this place.' This boded well so I boarded my plane in great anticipation.

But first I had to undergo the most spectacular flight I have ever been on. It was a relatively small plane so it flew low over the land and revealed scenes of valleys with meandering rivers – the largest being the impressive Yellow River -- then increasingly high mountain ranges, at first green with undergrowth then rapidly turning white with snow – and I gazed on a surreal winter wonderland which took my breath away. Finally the snow disappeared and was replaced with desert sands in many different hues of yellow, orange, pink, brown and grey. (This was the mountainous and desert route Xuanzang, the Chinese Buddhist monk and scholar, had travelled way back in the seventh century, on his way to India.) When we landed in the small Dunhuang airport at about 2.15pm I walked out into fresh, clean, unpolluted air – I had truly forgotten what that felt like.

I was already prepared to love this place and was further cheered by a buddha-like taxi driver who took my small case with a sweet smile and helped me into his taxi. I showed him the booking of the youth hostel on my phone and he knew it, so I settled down for the drive into town. The car windows were closed but I wanted more of that pristine air so I rolled down the one next to me. Even now I can't really put into words what happened next. It seemed as if a waft of peace, like a gentle breeze,

Flying low over the mountains to Dunhuang

wafted into the vehicle and I was infused with a deep softness and silence. As the journey progressed the feeling became stronger, and by the time I arrived at the youth hostel, I felt transparent, like I was floating in the air.

More goodies were to come. When I arrived Michael was right there, chatting to the manager whose apparent *tour de force* was making, he said, the best coffee in Dunhuang. A good cup of coffee was most acceptable and I sat down to enjoy it and hear about Michael's adventures which were no less splendid than mine. His train journey was an epic one of unusual experiences – a bit like travelling on Indian trains in the old days -- because the trains he travelled on were not the super-fast, modern bullet ones that connect major Chinese cities, but slow, winding, local ones which stopped at every small station. The scenery he saw was different to my views but equally stunning and he seemed to be as high in spirits as I was. It felt good that we were so in tune.

He and the manager then escorted me to my room which was simply adorable. After the very rough and primitive quarters I had been living in in Shilipu village, this charming little room, with its thoughtful touches, very nice shower room with constant hot water, and a western toilet, was welcome balm to my body and soul. I absolutely had not expected such comfortable, beautiful accommodation in a youth hostel. Michael was in a dormitory with three bunk beds which was also really nice and the manager, now having become his best friend, declined to put any other visitors into it so Michael had his own space for the duration of his time there. Things absolutely could not have been better.

We didn't waste much time, however, because we had one very important mission to accomplish: getting entrance tickets to view the Mogao Caves the following day. Our super-manager got a taxi for us and instructed the driver to take us to the office to buy the tickets.

The Mogao Caves are a World Heritage Site with thousands of tourists arriving every day so one had to book tickets ahead of time as there was a limit of six thousand tourists per day. The Chinese could book and pay online but it was acknowledged that western tourists didn't have this facility, so fortunately there were always tickets reserved for them.

Arriving at the office and while making arrangements, I was again struck by the softness and charm of the local people – very different from other parts of China. They were really sweet, kind and helpful. As foreigners we had to pay for a guide, and the cost also included visiting the maximum number of caves open for viewing. Preserving these caves is an international effort and extremely strict procedures are in place to protect them as they are very frail. Even the breath of so many visitors causes deterioration of the rock surfaces and damage to both paintings and sculptures. The state of all the caves is therefore very carefully monitored and they are open on a rotation basis, so the maximum number able to be viewed at any one time is twelve. The other caves are closed at this time.

One of the Mogao Caves (from a photograph in a Chinese book)

I did not see, for example, the huge reclining Buddha but, on the other hand, I did see two special ones, the second of which was of great importance to me. More of that later. While waiting for the tickets to be issued, I got into conversation with yet one more charming woman who spoke English. She was selling some books about the caves and I was fascinated by a beautifully illustrated Chinese book on display. Knowing that I would not be allowed to photograph any interiors of the caves, I asked her if I could photograph one of the pages. She obligingly held the book open while I took a photograph of a very richly decorated cave. To my joy I found that it was one of the ones I was able to enter the next day.

Having successfully completed our mission we went outside and explored some of the tourist shops nearby. When visiting a new place, it has always been my policy to look at some tourist shops because the souvenirs for sale unerringly display the chief attractions of the area. Here this policy did not fail me – because we found the dancing *apsaras* (*fei tien* in Chinese). Having had no previous knowledge of this colourful aspect of the Caves, we were intrigued. Gorgeous shawls, bags, postcards, pictures, fridge magnets … all depicted these wonderful *apsaras*: dancing, flying, heavenly spiritual beings who apparently lavishly decorate all the murals in the Caves. No seriousness here! These delightful entities – as well as the ubiquitous camels – are popular symbols of Dunhuang.

By this time, we were both tired and hungry (Michael had had almost no sleep the night before and I had left my village at 5.00 am to catch the train in Luoyang to get to Xi'an airport) so we set out for an early dinner at a Buddhist vegetarian restaurant Michael had found at lunchtime. This was another huge surprise. The stylish interior design and delicious, superbly-served food reminded me that we were in a World Heritage Site to which people came from all over the world and wanted service at a sophisticated level. Very beautiful local pottery and paintings were on display to enjoy or buy and the people were mellow and charming. There was a deep feeling of well-being and contentment.

This feeling continued when, on our way home, we briefly passed through the evening market, just starting to open up. The food part of it was hilarious in its bustle and busyness and the souvenir stalls were packed with goods of such colour, beauty and originality that we could hardly wait to return the following evening. But first, a good night's sleep was on the cards and soon, blissfully happy, I sank into sleep in my charming room, very much looking forward to continuing my quest to find the ten thousand buddhas the next morning.

കൽ

Our hostel manager had advised us to go early to the Mogao Caves Reception Centre because of the many tourists and long queues. So at the crack of dawn, I came downstairs to find Michael already there drinking the obligatory best-in-Dunhuang cup of coffee. I was quickly supplied with my own. Michael was chatting amiably with a man who I found out was a taxi driver, already procured for us by our super-manager. We were soon on our way but Michael had arranged for one important stop to be made: the *baozi* shop. I have mentioned these steamed buns (like *dim sum*) before. They are stuffed with both meat and vegetable fillings and can be very tasty and Michael and I frequented a special place in Dengfeng, but, he declared, the *baozi* here were far superior. On sampling them I enthusiastically agreed.

The sun was rising as we journeyed to the Mogao Reception Centre and I was again conscious of the soft peaceful energy that the streets seem to be suffused with. Nibbling our humble *baozi*, I thought maybe this was what manna from heaven tasted like.

Arriving at the Centre, with its customary statue of an apsara, I was hugely impressed with the design of the building. It was long and low with undulating curves, which, with its yellow/grey/brown colour, beautifully emulated the rolling desert sand dunes. Being early, we didn't have long to wait before being shepherded into a large cinema, holding the high-tech translating handsets with which we had been furnished. On the large screen we watched a detailed dramatisation of the Caves' history which gave us very helpful background information. But what came next was totally unexpected and utterly spectacular. On leaving the cinema we were shown into a huge space with a domed ceiling similar to a planetarium. When the lights dimmed, we started to see images of the interior of the Caves projected in clear detail and gorgeous colours onto the ceiling. It was incredible.

The Mogao Caves Reception Centre

An international consortium of experts oversees the preservation of the Caves, using as much scientific and technological know-how as possible in order to protect them and safeguard their priceless heritage. So no visitors are allowed to take photos inside the Caves, the lighting is low and natural – filtering in only from the entrance – and, because of so many people, one cannot linger at will to examine details; the guides have to keep people moving. Understanding all this, the organisers have had the interiors especially filmed and then projected onto the dome of the 'planetarium', placing us in a vast cave of virtual reality with a commentary, via the headsets, on what we were seeing. It was really a superb presentation and an extremely impressive, carefully executed way of ensuring that the visitor had the best possible experience of exploring the Caves while not risking any damage to them.

But the smooth efficiency and thoughtful attention to detail didn't end there. Emerging from the 'planetarium' we found a long line of luxury coaches waiting to transport us the twelve kilometres into the Gobi Desert to the site of the Caves.

Soon we were driving along a waterless river bed with cliffs increasing in size until caves cut into the hillside started to appear. At a bridge the coach stopped to deposit us and we duly took loads of photos and then started over the bridge to what was presumably our destination – currently hidden by tall trees. Instead of blinding sun and desert heat we walked into a cool avenue of greenery – that special feeling of being in a forest. Or was it something else? I tried to understand what I was feeling – because for sure this was hallowed ground. I am convinced there are places of special energy on the planet. Song Mountain is definitely one. Others could include Stonehenge and Canterbury Cathedral in England, certain temples and Arunachala in India, Bamiyan in Afghanistan... There are many, selected, I am sure by ancients who were more sensitive and aware than we are today. This place I was in now was definitely an energy site that the Buddhist monks had long ago discovered and then vastly enhanced by their meditation and devotion. I felt as if I was in a large open-air temple as I and Michael walked towards the entrance gates.

With the usual Chinese efficiency we were quickly pulled out of the long queue by a polite official and escorted to a waiting room where, he told Michael, an English-speaking guide would come and collect us.

While waiting for our guide I surveyed the scene in front of me. I had seen old photos of this hillside showing crumbling stone, exposed statues and broken walls, so I was struck by the skilled work that had been done to stabilise the hillside, re-enforce it and make walkways for the six thousand daily visitors, while still maintaining the character of the setting with aesthetic care, grace and thoughtfulness. Really, this was preservation of an ancient monument at its very best.

Then finally our guide arrived and I remain convinced to this day that we got the very best one. Tina was a beautiful university student who spoke excellent English and was doing a PhD in the history of Chinese Art. As we progressed on our tour, she revealed not only a vast knowledge of the historical facts of the Caves but also an obviously deep love and appreciation for the art in all its glorious aspects that she was telling us about. We had struck visitor gold!

We then started on the exploration of our allotted twelve caves. Each cave was closed with a metal door to prevent any unsupervised people entering, so Tina had a large key ring full of rather heavy keys. It was the third cave that hit me. It was probably the biggest of the caves we saw and as I entered, I was struck with such a strong energy hitting my heart that I gave an involuntary gasp and immediately bowed low to the huge Buddha image in front of me. Then, taking a step back I realised I had been fortunate to enter the very cave that I had the previous day taken a photo of in the book at the ticket office. Tina said that this was one of the most splendid and artistically important of all the caves; also one of the best preserved. I was overwhelmed at my good fortune at being here.

Walking further along the elevated passageway outside, Tina came to walk beside me and asked me why I was visiting the Caves. Possibly she was a little intrigued at my response in the previous cave. I told her about Osho and how his use of the phrase 'the ten thousand buddhas' had sent me on a path of discovery which had led me to these caves which I was certain were the origin of his words. She was very touched and interested and said she had never before had such an explanation shared with her.

Old caves dug into the cliffs

Walking to the entrance of the Caves

My lucky star was shining that day because, at the seventh cave we entered (officially Caves 16 and 17), I realised I was inside the only one I knew something about and was the one I most wanted to see. As I have mentioned before, the caves are open in rotation to preserve them as much as possible, so there is no knowing which ones a visitor will see. So when I walked into this one, I immediately recognised it and again drew an audible breath of excitement. Tina looked at me and smiled and asked, 'You know this one?' I replied, 'The Diamond Sutra! And Huineng's Platform Sutra!' She nodded her head and proceeded with the strange and fascinating history of this cave.

The building, decoration and worship of the Caves reached a peak in about the eleventh century after which they were abandoned and started to fall into ruin. I won't go into the subsequent history (it can all be found online) except for the astonishing discovery of caves 16 and 17 – because of its relevance to me. It seems that a monk called Hongbian carved out

Old photo by Sir Marc Aurel Stein of the Library Cave

a small cave (16) – which later became known as the Library Cave – just inside and next to the entrance of a bigger cave (17) as a kind of retreat place for himself. As the whole hillside fell into disrepair, somebody packed this small cave full of manuscripts left by monks, to preserve them, and then walled it off so it could not be seen and broken into, resulting in possible damage to the manuscripts and scrolls.

The cave was only discovered in 1900 by a monk, Wang Yuanlu, who had decided to try to do something to take care of the caves which had fallen into ruin. In 1907 he showed the Library Cave to the famous explorer, scientist and scholar, Sir Marc Aurel Stein. Searching through the stored documents, Stein immediately realised their profound historical value and decided to try to take some of them back to England. He was able to make a deal with Wang Yuanlu and brought many documents back home with him.

Amongst them was a printed copy of The Diamond Sutra, the world's oldest printed text, dated 868, and described by the British Library as 'the earliest complete survival of a dated printed book.'

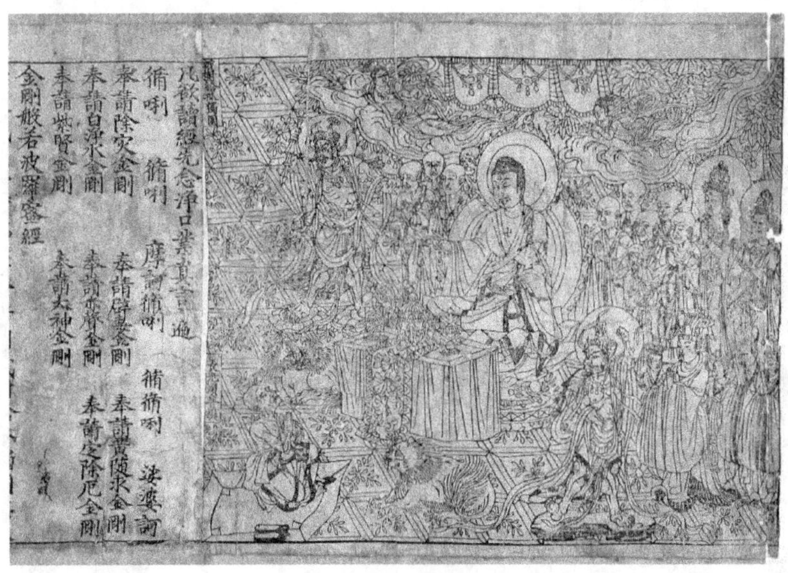

The Diamond Sutra

Also, copies of the Heart and Lotus Sutras were discovered and, of importance to those who love Zen, the only remaining copies of two versions of the Sixth Zen Patriarch Huineng's Platform Sutra, dated 830 and 860, were found. Such a treasure trove. I was thrilled to be able to see the exact place of these discoveries.

Of even further interest to me was the discovery in the Library Cave of four fragments of a text which are notes attributed to some unknown disciples of Bodhidharma. They consist of a question by a disciple and the answer by Bodhidharma. They were compiled, translated and edited by Nyogen Senzaki and Ruth Strout McCandless who then published a small book called *Buddhism and Zen* in New York in 1953. Osho used the translated fragments in this book as the basis for his discourses on Bodhidharma, published in book form as 'The White Lotus'.

In the first chapter of his book Osho says, *'These notes, fragmentary as they are, still are of great significance: they represent the essential core of Buddha's message.'*

Old photograph of the Caves as Sir Aurel Stein would have seen them
in 1907

Another old photograph

By the time we reached the last cave both Michael and I were rather overwhelmed with the rich artistic heritage we had seen as well as the very deep, strong, spiritual energy we could feel. Awesome! Mindblowing! Too much, in fact, to take in with one visit. The final stop on the tour was the viewing of the huge Buddha statue, so huge that it was impossible to see it properly from below. And we could not see it from afar because it was enclosed by the well-known current structure which is almost a symbol of the Mogao Caves. Tina said the statue is now the largest Buddha statue in the world since the Great Buddha in Bamiyan, Afghanistan, was tragically destroyed in 2001.

We were all profuse in our thanks to Tina for her very professional yet delightful and thought-provoking discourses. We wished we could have taken her for coffee or a meal to chat but she had to hurry back to take the next foreigners' tour.

Structure protecting the Great Buddha

Enjoying the luminous energy, Michael and I very slowly made our way to the coaches which would take us back to Dunhuang.

ॐ

Back at the hostel I told Michael I had to lie down in my room to try to sort out this profusion of buddhas. There were quite a few questions tumbling around in my head. Just what was the significance of 'ten thousand' of them? Why did Osho so insistently repeat that special phrase? Was he using the number as a symbol of collective devotion? Was it poetic license? Or was he simply being fairly prosaic: the more the merrier; the bigger the better!?

Perhaps a possible answer lies in something else he had often said. While sitting together in meditation with him, I remember him saying that the whole was greater than the sum of the individual parts. Remembering this, and reflecting on the grandeur and power of these Caves, it seemed to me that each one of the thousands of painted and carved Buddhas embodied the devoted heart of a seeker, looking to drop the petty considerations of the ego and fly into the realms of the unknown far greater than the small, individual self. Maybe a meaning similar to the one described by the young monk in the Xiantong Temple in Wutai Shan.

We can never really know, but perhaps Osho was evoking a connection with the ancients by pointing a finger – possibly an enlightening one – at their understanding to help us, his beloved present-day people on the path.

࿐

The Chinese give wonderfully imaginative names to natural phenomena and the place we were going to visit on the following day was rather romantically known as 'The Singing Sands'.

On the edge of the town a cluster of sand dunes surround an oasis of water, shaped like a crescent moon. For over two thousand years this lake has never dried up nor changed its shape – until recently. Of course, modern life, an increasing population and land use have taken the expected toll, but fortunately measures were taken about thirty years ago to protect the oasis and, although diminished, it is still beautifully impressive.

We have heard about how desert sands continually shift and change form due to the wind, and so it is uniquely unusual for dunes to stay the same shape and for the oasis not to disappear over time. Scientific research has concluded that, because the Mingsha Mountain ranges on the southern and northern sides of the crescent lake are much higher than the mountains on the eastern and western sides, the winds blow the sand in a certain way which prevent the sand from covering the lake and also prevent the sand dunes from radically changing shape. Nature is amazing.

After a relatively later *baozi* breakfast the following day, Michael and I grabbed a taxi and joined the other tourists to explore these very striking natural wonders close to Dunhuang. The road actually just ended suddenly at the first looming sand dune, at the base of which a row of camels plodded along bearing their load of tourists. I know it was a tourist attraction but still there was something very picturesque and timeless seeing these animals, symbols of so many desert adventures, up close.

The immediate dune behind them was pristine sand, but as we walked around its base, the next one was heavily indented with footprints – because of course, the next thing a tourist has to do is climb up the dune. This was a feat too far for me but Michael immediately started to climb. He was wearing his soft kungfu cloth shoes, so he had decided not to use the bright orange cloth boots given out free of charge to the tourists to prevent their own shoes being filled with the very soft, fine sand.

I set off for the crescent lake which had been one of my dreams to see. It truly did not disappoint. It is hard to explain… All one can see is yellow sand and blue sky and then suddenly, in the middle of it all, is this blue lake with an ancient temple beside it. Fortunately, there were not too many people around so I was able to experience it as it must have looked many hundreds of years ago.

I have long been fascinated with the history of the Silk Road and all that happened along its way, so I felt a tug of something very ancient when I stood silently trying to absorb the scene. Again, I was aware of some magical soft energy hovering over the place despite some chattering tourists and wailing kids behind me.

There was a path between the lake and the temple which I followed and found a good-sized tree under which a gnarled wooden bench had been placed. Perfect to sit on and contemplate, and wait for Michael. Reading the ever-present information boards in appalling English, this was apparently a very unique tree which can exist in extremely arid conditions. I also learned why the sands sing. It seems that the sand grains here have a certain physical formation which make sounds like singing or sighing when moved and rubbed against each other by winds or footsteps. Michael said he could distinctly hear the sounds when he climbed over the first dune and up the next one where there were no people.

Eventually he appeared at the top of the first dune and made his way downhill, half walking, half sliding. He was utterly thrilled at the experience of surmounting the second dune – he said he felt like he was the only person on the planet – total silence, total nothingness.

Certainly, our trip here was one of infinitely unusual and otherworldly experiences.

The crescent-moon shaped oasis

As we were both famished, we decided to return to the hostel for a snack and a break – I needed a nap and Michael wanted to explore the town and shops. We planned to have a big meal in the Night Market as a farewell celebration because we were leaving the following day.

Unlike most men who abhor shopping, Michael was a shopping buff, so that evening we made our way to the food via the souvenir stalls to buy presents to take back for friends. Dengfeng is a dismal shopping area with a total lack of anything attractive to buy. Dunhuang, on the other hand was an absolute treasure trove of delightful curios – many hand-crafted ones – artistic, colourful, original and cheap.

The day before we had eaten at the delightful Buddhist vegetarian restaurant, but this time we chose the Night Market simply because it was so much fun! I mean, if you could order a Banquet in Silver Paper, or Glutinous Rice Soup, or Haggis, or Spirit Immortal Gruel … why wouldn't you? Again, the locals were fascinated with a westerner who could speak good Chinese and joke and play with them, so we were welcomed at whatever cooking stall we visited. They were, in turn, delighted to share their cuisine with us.

৯৽৶

On my journey home to Song Mountain, reflecting on all I and Michael had experienced, it seemed to me that, from the ten thousand buddhas in the nearby Mogao Caves, a mantle of Buddhahood spread softly over the town of Dunhuang and its people. It felt like we had entered a realm of beauty, grace and timelessness. Is it possible that this is the state of consciousness to which Osho was pointing with his so often repeated phrase? I truly think so.

11
Sacred Emptiness

Full Moon over Song Mountain[7]

Zen is just Zen.
There is nothing comparable to it.
It is unique – unique in the sense
that it is the most ordinary
and yet the most extraordinary phenomenon
that has happened to human consciousness.
It is the most ordinary because
it does not believe in knowledge,
it does not believe in mind.
It is not a philosophy, not a religion either.
It is the acceptance of the ordinary existence
with a total heart, with one's total being.
It has no interest in any esoteric nonsense,
no interest in metaphysics at all.
It does not hanker for the other shore;
this shore is more than enough.
Its acceptance of this shore is so tremendous
that through that very acceptance
it transforms this shore…
and this very shore becomes the other shore.

Osho

Sacred Emptiness

Whereas in western countries, bricks for buildings are made mostly of sand or clay with a bit of cement mixed in, bricks in China are made from solid concrete. The result is that in the summer, the bricks heat up and retain the heat so that the interiors of most houses are like an oven – particularly if you are on the top floor where the roof is flat. Conversely, in winter, the bricks literally freeze and one feels like one is living in a fridge. The concept of insulation and double glazing seemingly has not yet been widely adopted in China.

Without even ceilings installed for some basic insulation, and with the ill-fitting windows generously allowing the whistling winter wind ready access at all times, my cavernous concrete top-floor 'penthouse' was unbearably cold.

In addition, the damp, impenetrable fog for which this area is notorious, had descended on us like a thick quilt – and stayed. Its heavy, chilly tendrils seeped into every corner of my establishment, denying all the efforts of my small heater, three hot water bottles and thermal underwear to save me from being chilled to the very marrow.

Then Yujie called me from Beijing. She told me that she had seen the news that central Henan Province was experiencing exceptionally cold weather and wondered if I wanted to come and stay with her and her husband and little boy. They had recently moved into a new apartment with a nice spare room and the place was toasty warm.

Furthermore, she was planning a four-day trip to Shanghai to supervise work on her new branch office there. Being further south and on the coast, Shanghai was much warmer than Beijing and Song Mountain. Perhaps I would like to come with her and visit Ibo and Tina? She said she had already contacted them and they were enthusiastic about a farewell visit. Loath as I was to miss a minute of my time on the mountain, it was obvious that remaining there would become increasingly difficult and that she was providing the perfect rescue operation. So I gratefully accepted.

Yujie instantly switched into business mode and told me that because she needed to make many arrangements we should decide immediately on a departure date so she could book train tickets. I thought quickly and suggested three days later. There was silence while she scrolled through available train times on her phone, came up with two convenient options, one of which I chose, and just like that, she had booked our trip on the spot! I still blinked a bit at how things moved at lightning speed in China.

The Wu family were a little shocked at these sudden departure plans but could see the practicalities involved and right away set about arranging a farewell dinner. Wenju would take me to the train station in Zhengzhou, just over an hour's drive away.

The remaining few days were a flurry of packing and goodbyes. Although for me it was certain that I wouldn't return, my lovely friends were already saying, 'See you in the Spring' because they expected me to come back again then as I had done for so many years before. None of us had any intimation of the devastating bomb that would explode within two or three months in the form of the Covid virus nor how it would affect the whole world and life as we had known it up until now.

Surprisingly, I felt no sorrow at leaving this most special place and these very precious people that I loved so dearly. Simply the time had come when it was right to leave. I felt replete, fulfilled and content. Nothing more was needed. Everything was perfectly complete. I felt that the mountain and its people were so embedded in my soul that it was impossible to feel any kind of separation.

༄༅

Visiting the silent Zhongyue Miao Temple frequently, and meditating there during my many visits, I felt I had touched upon some essence of Taoism, which had originally been an essential influence on Zen.

With my quest to find the meaning hidden in Osho's frequent references to the 'ten thousand buddhas' during the few years before his death, and through the myriad levels of communication with Yujie and her family, and with Ibo and Tina – all of whom were devout Buddhists – I had experienced something of the essence of Buddhism.

But of greater consequence for me was connecting so deeply with Master Wu Nanfang, his family, and his Gulun Kungfu, all suffused with the legacy of 'the greatest Zen master, Bodhidharma', and the energy of the extraordinary Song Mountain. For them Zen was most certainly present in everyday life, not something to be practised in a temple. And because of them, my own understanding of Zen as revealed to me through all the years of sitting at the feet of Osho – my own incomparable Zen Master – had been deepened and confirmed.

As he so often does, Osho says it best:

Zen goes beyond Buddha and beyond Lao Tzu.
It is a culmination, a transcendence,
both of the Indian genius and of the Chinese genius.
The Indian genius reached its highest peak in Gautam the Buddha
and the Chinese genius reached its highest peak in Lao Tzu.

And the meeting…
the essence of Buddha's teaching and the essence of Lao Tzu's teaching
merged into one stream so deeply that no separation is possible now.
Even to make a distinction between what belongs to Buddha
and what to Lao Tzu is impossible, the merger has been so total.
It is not only a synthesis; it is an integration.
Out of this meeting Zen was born.
Zen is neither Buddhist nor Taoist and yet both.

To call Zen 'Zen Buddhism' is not right because it is far more.
Buddha is not as earthly as Zen is; Lao Tzu is tremendously earthly,
but Zen is not only earthly: its vision transforms the earth into heaven.
Lao Tzu is earthly, Buddha is unearthly,
Zen is both –
and in being both,
it has become the most extraordinary phenomenon.

അം

In the last years before he died, Osho's discourses were almost exclusively on Zen. He also introduced a meditation at the end of each discourse where he guided us – his ten thousand buddhas – into a profoundly silent inner space: a direct transmission of Zen.

It was as if his intent was to show us that, although he talked with such insight and inspiration on so many different paths to reveal their intrinsic essence and significance, in the end it was Zen which most closely conveyed his essential final message. I remember the tears streaming down my face when, shortly before he stopped talking, he used Basho's evocative Zen poem as a way to try to express that which is ultimately inexpressible:

> *We can sit in silence and listen to the birds or the wind in the trees.*
> *'Just sitting silently, doing nothing,*
> *the spring comes and the grass grows by itself.'*
> *That is going to be my ultimate message and my final work on earth.*

Although he is no longer here in physical form, his presence remains in every cell of my body, in the very core of my being. And it is with the deepest gratitude and the greatest joy that I continue on the way he has revealed to me – a Zen way of silent, sacred emptiness which reflects the infinite fullness of existence.

Acknowledgements

Very many thanks to:

Dhiren Townley – without whom this book would probably not have been written – at least in its current form. He is the 'editor supreme', the one with the eagle eye which notices errors of all kinds and suggests how to fix them; whose intrinsic love and command of the English language means he can intuitively suggest different or better ways of saying something when I don't get it quite right; who joins in the huge fun of discovering unknown facts, relevant poetic verses, obscure but meaningful historical and spiritual references; who shares his more informed knowledge and also understanding of fields different to mine … all of which has added enormously to the texture and richness of my book which hopefully many readers will enjoy.

Gopa & Ted2, Inc. – who, having spent twenty or more years of professionally designing books and book covers, have designed a cover for me which is personal, yet beautifully conveys the essence of my book. It has a Zen simplicity, and uses one of their paintings which echoes the desert mountains in which many Buddhist caves were carved. The painting is one I had very much admired in the past and I am very honoured that they have chosen to use it for my book cover. The whole concept is simply perfect.

Yujie Zhou – who, because she speaks such good English, was a window into the Chinese world for me, and also the 'go-to' person when I needed help or information in so many different circumstances; for example, missing planes or trains, getting dental treatments when the dentists spoke no English, needing a place to stay… Being fond of travel herself, she also took me to exotic places like Hohhot in Inner Mongolia, Hainan Island in the South China Seas and Suzhou, home of both the original Japanese gardens and the Chinese silk heritage. Her very considerable knowledge and understanding of Chinese Buddhist and Zen traditions was of huge interest and help to me.

Ibo Fei – who died so tragically last year at such a young age – 34 years – from an incurable liver condition. His determination not to let his illness get in the way of living his life to the full was an ongoing inspiration, and the observations of his quick, keen, intelligent mind often left me in awe. Above all, his sense of humour and ability to crack jokes in English, a foreign language to him, kept me laughing whenever we were together and even when separated by oceans. I will never forget him and will miss him always.

Master Wu Nanfang, his wife, his son, Wenju, and his daughter, Lijuan – without whose kind, thoughtful and generous support, I would not have been able to have stayed in China in the enormously rewarding way that I did. Master Wu Nanfang took it upon himself to show me local places of his childhood and tell me fascinating stories of his kungfu ancestors who form part of the rich spiritual and historical traditions of the Song Mountain area. As he spoke no English, it was his daughter, Lijuan, who did most of the translating, for which I am forever grateful. And Wenju drove me here, there, and everywhere in assorted vehicles, often of dubious origin. But the family's greatest gift to me was sharing their lives lived in a simple and meditative Zen way – by being with them, observing them, I learnt some very deep lessons for which I am eternally grateful.

YaJun, ChenGeng, Helen and Tina – who have so often answered my questions about many Chinese-related topics and sent me many interesting Chinese photos, old and new, which enhance my book and online media sites.

The villagers in Shilipu village – especially my landlords, Mr and Mrs Shang, and Xiaofeng, my good friend at the convenience store… All these warm-hearted, local people were friendly and kind and accepted me unreservedly as one of them, despite my foreignness and the lack of language. Getting to know them and their local village lives was a unique and treasured experience.

And to my brother and his wife, and so many good friends around the globe, too many to mention individually – who have helped me in various ways such as finding small but important pieces of information on various topics, advising me on areas about which I am not very familiar, and generally supporting me by calling or emailing me, invariably at exactly the right moment … which brightened my days and spurred me onwards.

Appendix 1 – UNESCO Information

*The decision to make the Song Mountain area a World Heritage
Site due to its 'outstanding universal value'
... from the UNESCO website*

For many centuries Dengfeng, one of the early capitals of China whose precise location is unknown, but whose name is now associated with an area to the south of Mount Shaoshi and Mount Taishi, two peaks of Mount Songshan, came to be associated with the concept of the centre of heaven and earth – the only point where astronomical observations were considered to be accurate. The natural attribute of the centre of heaven and earth was seen to be Mount Songshan and worship of Mount Songshan was used by the emperors as a way of reinforcing their power.

The three ideas do therefore converge to some extent: the centre of heaven and earth in astronomical terms is used as a propitious place for a capital of terrestrial power, and Mount Songshan, as the natural symbol of the centre of heaven and earth, is used as the focus for sacred rituals that reinforce that earthly power. The buildings that clustered around Dengfeng were of the highest architectural standards when built and many were commissioned by Emperors. They thus reinforced the influence of the Dengfeng area.

Some of the sites in the nominated area relate closely to the mountain (Zhongyue Temple, Taishi Que and Shaoshi Que); the Observatory is very clearly associated with the astronomical observations made at the centre of heaven and earth, while the remainder of the buildings were built in the area perceived to be the centre of heaven and earth – for the status that this conferred.

Mount Songshan is considered to be the central sacred mountain of China. At the foot of this 1500-metre-high mountain, close to the city of

Dengfeng in Henan province and spread over a 40 square-kilometre circle, stand eight clusters of buildings and sites, including three Han Que gates (remains of the oldest religious edifices in China), many temples, the Zhougong Sundial Platform and the Dengfeng Observatory. Constructed over the course of nine dynasties, these buildings are reflections of different ways of perceiving the centre of heaven and earth and the power of the mountain as a centre for religious devotion. The historical monuments of Dengfeng include some of the best examples of ancient Chinese buildings devoted to ritual, science, technology and education.

Appendix 2 – About Dengfeng

Song Mountain is considered to be the central sacred mountain of China. At the foot of this 1500-metre-high mountain lies the city of Dengfeng. The city's original name was Yangcheng but its name was changed by the Empress Wu Zetian (624 – 705) who, although living in the capital city of Luoyang, loved visiting the mountain and Dengfeng. She was a devoted Buddhist (it is said that the famous Buddha in the Longmen Caves in Luoyang, was built in her likeness) and in 696 she held a grand sacrificial ceremony on the top of Song Mountain to give thanks and pay tribute to its sacred powers and to declare it the spiritual centre of heaven and earth.

The meaning of Dengfeng is as follows: 'deng' means 'to ascend' and 'feng' means 'to hold a grand sacrificial ceremony'. Or, in other translations: 'Ascending to bestow honour'.

Dengfeng was considered to be the centre of ancient China, and it served as the capital and cultural centre for many dynasties. For as long as three thousand years, students of Confucianism, Buddhism, Taoism – and later Zen – settled here to devote themselves to their spiritual practices in the rare spiritual ambience of the mountain. Many shrines, structures and temples – many still standing to this day – were built, reflecting the persistent tradition of this area as being the 'Centre of Heaven and Earth'. Dengfeng therefore has been of great importance in Chinese culture.

Today, it is better known as the home of the Shaolin Temple and the birthplace of kungfu martial arts.

One lesser known, yet very significant fact – adding to Dengfeng's mystique of being the 'centre of Heaven and Earth' – is the existence of the Gaocheng Observatory to the south east of the city. It is China's oldest and best-preserved observatory. Its present structure dates as far back as the thirteenth century with, however, ruined remains which indicate that the site was in even earlier use. Ever since ancient times, Chinese people had believed that the world has a centre. And, according to historical scientific knowledge, the specific measurements of the shadows of the structure of this Observatory meant that it was classified for thousands of years as the centre of the world.

Appendix 3
'Walnut Season on Song Mountain'

After hearing from Veena about the walnut trees on Song Mountain in China, Dhiren Townley was inspired to write this poem:

Walking back down from the slopes of the mountain,
this morning, maybe I missed the walnut trees,
maybe I was quiet, wrapped in the ancient autumns,
and maybe the smiles of a hundred hungry hermits,
once in walnut season,
who had passed this way
and glimpsed out of the corner of my inner eye:
they'd led me here,
where this old lady cracking walnuts in the afternoon sun,
smiles at me and calls me over,
here in the shade of Song Mountain.

Foraging and blessing, tired and happy....
I can see them still, in the mind's eye,
carrying herbs and flowers, walnuts spiced
and diced and cured into herbal medicine,
soups and sauces, pickles: winter food.
They stop and smile and eyes still
twinkling, bless me as I sit;
they shimmer, coming down
from Bodhidharma's cave,
and seem to smile out loud,
here in the shade of Song Mountain.

And as we sit, on this warm wall as it sinks into the evening light,
her village friends come by to husk and crack and gather,
and to meet her visitor, fresh from somewhere else,
and so we talk, without the tiresome need
of some known lingua franca.
Maybe we are talking about the *wu wei wu,*
and why Bodhidharma came to the East,
or of the weather and the harvest,
but to me, it seems, we are quite happily
chatting together about walnut season,
here in the shade of Song Mountain.

Bibliography

Osho: *Ah This!, Bodhidharma, the Greatest Zen Master, The White Lotus* (Rebel Publishing)
Bill Porter: *Zen Baggage* (Counterpoint, Berkley, USA)
Andy Ferguson: *Tracking Bodhidharma, Zen's Chinese Heritage'* (Wisdom Publications, Boston, USA)
Susan Whitefield: *Aurel Stein on the Silk Road* (The British Museum Press, London UK)

Notes

1 -- *miao* means a temple with a shrine and/or fair. During the autumn of each year there has been a huge market or fair in Zhongyue Miao for many hundreds of years. And of course it is famous for the Taoist shrine which has been there in one form or another since 700 BC

2 – Chiyono was a Japanese Abbess and the first female Zen master in the Rinzai School of Zen, who became enlightened in the Kaizo-ji Temple in Kamakura. After her enlightenment she wrote this poem:

> *This way and that, I tried to keep the pail together,*
> *hoping the weak bamboo would never break.*
> *Suddenly the bottom fell out.*
> *No more water,*
> *no more reflections of the full moon in the water –*
> *emptiness in my hand.*

3 – see Ch 10 for more information.

4 – see *A Mountain in China*, Ch 3, page 107

5 – CCTV 4's documentary on Master Wu Nanfang and Gulun Kungfu: https://www.youtube.com/watch?v=gddEOAr35zE

6 – for the full translation of the text please see: http://tinyurl.com/2p8w9rba

7 – the photograph of the full moon was taken by the author on a Song Mountain peak

Media Links

https://3booksblog.wordpress.com/
www.instagram.com/booksbyveena
for many coloured photos illustrating *Farewell to Song Mountain*
www.facebook.com/booksbyveena
www.amazon.com/veenaschlegel
www.amountaininchina8.com
for many coloured photos illustrating *A Mountain in China*

☙❧

About the Author

Veena Schlegel was born and brought up in South Africa but left at the age of twenty-one, never to return. She has travelled extensively throughout the world, spending more than half of her adult life in eastern countries: India, Japan and China.

She has self-published four books: *A Vanished Road* – about her journey overland to India in the early seventies; *Glimpses of my Master* – about spending twenty years as a disciple of the eastern mystic, Osho; *A Mountain in China* – about her life in a small village in China and her personal Zen quest; *Gulun Kungfu* – about a little-known, traditional style of kungfu, practised only in the Song Mountain area.